ENCOUNTERS
--- WITH ---
WISDOM

ENCOUNTERS
--- WITH ---
WISDOM

BOOK SIX

Thomas Hora, M. D.

The PAGL Foundation

www.pagl.org

Published by the PAGL Foundation

www.pagl.org

The PAGL Foundation
c/o Robert Wieser
21 Talcott Road
Rye Brook, New York 10573

Manufactured in the United States of America.

ISBN 13: 978-0-913105-24-5
ISBN 10: 0-913105-24-4

Contents

═══   ═══

Editors' Preface

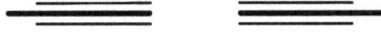

This book presents dialogues between Dr. Thomas Hora, psychiatrist, spiritual teacher, and founder of Existential Metapsychiatry, and some of his students. They occurred in the late 1980s through 1995. Dr. Hora recorded most of the group sessions with his students, and made them available to those who attended. The PAGL Foundation[1] has collected many of these tapes and transcribed them. For the reader new to the teachings of Metapsychiatry, it is suggested that these dialogues will be more meaningful if one of Dr. Hora's other books, especially *Beyond the Dream*, is read first.

Dr. Hora maintained his practice in his homes (an apartment in New York City and a house in Bedford, New York). Group sessions were held in the living room, where chairs were arranged in a circle. After the students had gathered, Dr. Hora would enter and sit down. He greeted each student non-verbally with eye contact and a smile, and then he waited for a question to be asked. If no question was forthcoming, Dr. Hora opened the dialogue.

Metapsychiatry values the sincere question, and Dr. Hora always waited for students to formulate questions. He listened for their sincerity as this indicated a student's receptivity and desire to understand. Sometimes a question might be phrased in an awkward or convoluted way. In such instances some of the meandering has been edited here for the sake of clarity.

As a dialogue progressed, there could be long silences or pauses. At such times Dr. Hora might introduce an entirely new topic, perhaps

---

1 - PAGL is an acronym for Peace, Assurance, Gratitude, and Love, qualities of consciousness that are the fruit of spiritual progress. The PAGL Foundation was established to make Dr. Hora's work available (*see www.PAGL.org*).

discerning an unasked question. He also saw and was amused by the paradoxes that life offered, and shared this often in asides and humorous remarks. He showed his students how to laugh at their woes by lifting their vision to a higher perspective, helping them make the distinction between taking something seriously vs. giving it full attention. Laughter erupted frequently.

Overall, the editors have chosen to keep the flow of the dialogue as it occurred, so that no major changes have been made other than to maintain the anonymity of the participants and improve readability. Although some of the ideas in these dialogues may have been addressed in various ways in other available materials, to the sincere student, the freshness of these sessions can offer new insights and reinforce old ones.

* * *

June, 2019

1

The Anti-Christ

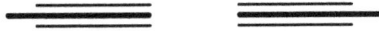

Student: What is motivation?

Dr. Hora: Motivation is a certain thought that governs our choices and decisions and actions. It is a thought.

Student: Is it a kind of an umbrella thought that leads us to certain actions, responses, decisions?

Dr. Hora: Umbrella? I don't know if it's an "umbrella." It's just a thought. Hitler had a thought that certain races and groups of people were inferior to his own, and therefore had to be extinguished. He had this thought, and this thought motivated him to fantastic actions and results. Now, if somebody lives with the right motives, he is the "right man," and the right man cannot do wrong; but if the motive is the wrong motive, then whatever he will do will be disastrous. [1] So the issue of motive is very important.

Student: Is motive equivalent to our interest?

Dr. Hora: Not equivalent. An interest can then *create* the motive. If we are interested in good and beauty and harmony, then we are motivated to move around in the world in such a way that there will be harmony, beauty, love, and intelligent coexistence. Interest determines the motive.

It is unbelievable that there may be people who are interested in evil

---

1 - "There is a Taoist saying, 'If the right man does the wrong thing, then the wrong thing will work the right way; but if the wrong man does the right thing, then the right thing will work the wrong way.'" *Beyond the Dream, Session No. 11.*

and then, without realizing it, can generate problems in the world and their lives. If we come to consider motives, we can ask this question: "Is there a devil?" Frequently people say as a joke, "The devil made me do it!" We laugh, but it is not a laughing matter. We must really understand the devil. Some people will say, "That's nonsense. There is no devil."

The question is, do we understand what people mean by "the devil?" Some people mean one thing, others another. Of course students of Metapsychiatry are not religious; but it is appropriate for us to ask the question, "Is there a devil?" If there is a devil, where does he come from? who is he? what is he? What is the importance of recognizing the existence of a devil or ignoring him as an old wives' tale? It's a rather interesting issue.

When we speak about the devil, we usually have some kind of individual in mind who is malicious and walks about with a pitchfork with three prongs; but we cannot say that there is "a devil" as such. That is religious superstition. But we *can* say that there are *invalid motivations* that govern certain individual consciousnesses.

Student: Could you say, then, that it would be like a devilish thought? Like what Hitler was entertaining was an invalid, devilish thought?

Dr. Hora: Absolutely. Of course.

Student: Sometimes even we can be stuck with a thought and know it's invalid.

Dr. Hora: And there are some people who become very malicious, and they are not aware of it. If you say, "You are being malicious," they would deny it. "Who, me? I am a nice guy!" Right? There are many different devils. It is safe to say that we can look around the world and see many kinds of devils that motivate people's perceptions, reactions and influences, and they may not recognize that this is so. In Metapsychiatry, we are particularly interested in a special devil, which is called the "anti-Christ." What is this devil that is called the anti-Christ? Have you ever heard of the anti-Christ? What is it?

Student: Would that be self-confirmatory thinking?

Dr. Hora: No. The self-confirmatory thinker is also afflicted by some devilish thought, but it is more self-promotion. He doesn't have to be a malicious individual. He is just interested in himself, to promote himself and to impress people. This is not the anti-Christ. Self-confirmation is the source of difficulties, and we know that people get sick from bragging, bullshitting, etc. But in Metapsychiatry, we are interested quite a bit in the phenomenon called the anti-Christ. What makes us interested in this special thing, the anti-Christ? It is because Metapsychiatry has its solid foundation in Christly values. What are Christly values?

Student: Spiritual values.

Dr. Hora: Spiritual values like what?

Student: Joy—gratitude —

Another Student: love—assurance—

Other Students: beauty —harmony — peace—freedom —wisdom…

Dr. Hora: Yes, *everything* in Metapsychiatry is based on Christly values. Therefore, the devil in the form of an anti-Christ is of great interest to us. We are very interested in that. We can enumerate Christly values, and everyone seems to agree that it is a good thing. Christly values are good values, and we call them "existentially valid values." What does that mean?

Student: It means that they promote a good life, a healthy life.

Dr. Hora: Exactly. Everything beautiful, intelligent, and true is contained in the Christly value system. Now here comes the devil, and he says, "That is ridiculous. What are you, a religious nut, that you should be interested in Christly values? Don't you see that the world is full of hostility, deception, malice, anger, negativity, murder, and mayhem?" The world is ruled by the anti-Christ, with all the values that deny Reality and the validity of Christly values. If you appreciate Christly values, people will say that you are a fool, that you live in a fool's paradise. It appears that the world is ruled by everything *except* the Christ. This anti-Christ is king in the world, and it seems that everybody is an enemy to the Christly value system. You look around and you see malicious people, you see criminals, you see violence, you see all kinds of values that are the opposite of the Christ. The world seems to be full of the anti-Christ. There seem to be more evil people in the world and negative thinkers than enlightened people who are loving and constructive and beneficial presences.

To us in Metapsychiatry, the phenomenon of the anti-Christ is very important. It is not a religious thing. It is an existential dilemma that we cannot just hide ourselves from or run away from or close our eyes to and say, "This is not true; this is not real; it is nothing; we don't have to be concerned with this devil or the anti-Christ."

How can we account for the seeming existence of the devil?

Student: The devil seems to exist as a consequence of the tendency to judge by appearances. The world seems to be filled with danger and problems and threats. It's promoted by the media. We are inundated by these suggestions all the time.

Dr. Hora: Right. So, are we foolish to devote our energies and attentions to the Christly value system and to be guided by it? Wouldn't it be smarter if we were to just join the anti-Christ forces and be bitchy and evil and criminal and get away with things in order to prove that those who appreciate Christly values are stupid?

Student: When you suffer the consequences of following worldly values, then you have an incentive to follow Christly values.

Dr. Hora: What if you don't suffer? What if you prosper? The Mafia people prosper. It's complicated. It's not that clear. There are anti-Christ individuals who seemingly get away with murder.

Student: And greed—apparently greed is profitable.

Dr. Hora: That's what makes it more difficult for Metapsychiatry to focus on the Christ. These people might say, "What do you mean, 'Christ?' Are you crazy? Look at how people live who are against this nonsense!"

Student: Like lambs among wolves.

Dr. Hora: Could you explain that?

Student: It seems that if you subscribe to the Christly values, it's sort of a nonaggressive, gentle approach, and you seem to be open to people who are very aggressive or violent or crafty or manipulative. You can be victimized in certain ways.

Dr. Hora: But the wolves are much stronger than the lambs, and they are smarter, and the lamb seems to be stupid; so why should we bother studying Christliness?

Student: Sometimes out of the sense of human decency.

Dr. Hora: What is that?

Student: This negative, vicious way of living, it's there and it's prevalent, but you don't want to give in to it, to live that way, out of a sense of what's right and wrong—what's decent.

Dr. Hora: But it brings you money and good-looking chicks. (*Laughter*) You can have a ball!

Student: It's underhanded, it's dirty, it's immoral.

Dr. Hora: Now you are moralizing, and this is particularly objectionable to certain people. There are many who would say, "Only 'stupid' people are moral; the 'smart' people are smart, and it is stronger to be smart than to be Christlike." This is a very complicated situation, and we have to ask ourselves, are we really interested in the Christly way of life or would we enjoy the anti-Christ's way of life better?

Student: But the Bible says, "As ye sow, so shall ye reap."[2] If that's the way of the anti-Christ, then that doesn't seem so good.

Dr. Hora: That is not just the way of the anti-Christ. The Christly way is sowing *good* seeds. The anti-Christ way is sowing *bad* seeds, and as ye sow, so shall ye reap. You can reap good fruit by sowing Christly seeds. This does not explain the mystery of the anti-Christ.

Student: We say we are making an effort toward being Christlike, but secretly we are interested in the anti-Christ. We are going in two different directions. It's like straddling a fence. It's not a case of the Christ or the anti-Christ; it's a case of managing both. (*Laughter*)

Dr. Hora: Oh! So, this student has come up with a solution! How does this help with solving this dilemma? A little bit of this and a little bit of that. This is called religious hypocrisy. Do we recommend this? (*Laughter*)

Student: I don't recommend it, but it's better than being the anti-Christ.

Dr. Hora: What's wrong with being the anti-Christ?

Student: It's a dog-eat-dog kind of existence.

Dr. Hora: Could you explain that?

Student: If you suspect that everybody is out to get you, you need to be stronger and smarter and more manipulative than they are. Then when you come into a situation, you are trying to figure out what he or she is doing so you can maneuver to a good position. This is the way you live. It's not a good way to live.

Dr. Hora: It's not good? It sounds very good when you describe it. (*Laughter*)

Student: Can Christly values be dualistic?

Dr. Hora: What is your problem with that?

---

2 - "Be not deceived; God is not mocked: for whatsoever a man soweth, that shall he also reap." (Galatians 6:7)

Student: The way this is coming across, evil is the dual side of good—the flip side.

Dr. Hora: Real good has no flip side.

Student: I know. The way this anti-Christ is being put forth, it's like it's in the dualistic realm, and that kind of realm is not valid.

Dr. Hora: But the anti-Christ can play the role of the good. That is where he gets you. He says, "Listen. I tell you clearly that there are good aspects to being anti-Christ." Right? So the anti-Christ value system is good *and* bad. The Christly value system is only good. That is the devilish thing in it, because the devil can be very generous and give you powers.

Do you know the play *Faust* by Goethe? Faust was a scientist extremely interested in the powers that scientific knowledge could give him. He was very ambitious. He wanted to have so much knowledge of scientific facts, that the devil spotted him and came to him and said, "I can offer you a deal you can't refuse. What do you want?" The scientist said, "I want to have such power through science that I can rule the world." The devil said, "I can arrange that. I'll take some blood from your finger, and we'll draw up a contract, and I will give you all the power of science that you crave, and you will indeed be famous! You will get the Nobel Prize, you will impress the whole world with your knowledge for a certain period of time—six months or so—but then you must come back and you will be my slave forever. As long as you live, you will serve me." So, Faust signed the contract, and then his life evolved into horrendous suffering. After a while everything collapsed, and he began to see his error and prayed for redemption. We won't go into that here. It's an old story and has been presented in many forms.

The anti-Christ as the devil can come to us and offer us spurious forms of power, happiness, possessions, money and women—whatever your heart desires. The devil can give it to you, which means, if you are interested in these things, then you can experience them.

It is a great problem in human life when the devil, the anti-Christ, can show you it is good to be on its side.

Student: In the Bible, we are told that Christ was tempted with three temptations.[3] He understood how to transcend them. Do we have to go through those temptations too?

Dr. Hora: Definitely. If we are interested in reaching Christ consciousness, we are going to.

The devil told Jesus, "You can do anything because you are a favorite son of God. You have been in the desert now for 40 days; you haven't had anything to eat. Why don't you take this big rock and turn it into bread so you won't be hungry? You can do it because you are the son of God." So, what did Jesus say?

Student: "Man does not live by bread alone."

Dr. Hora: Yes, he always refuted the anti-Christ. We do that all the time, right? More or less successfully. (*Laughter*) So he said to the devil, "Man does not live by bread alone, but by every word which proceedeth out of the mouth of God." Jesus passed this test, and then the devil said, "You are such a great guy, and people don't know it. Why don't you climb up on a high tower, or something, and throw yourself down? Show the folks that nothing will happen to you because God will come like Superman and catch you and you will not get hurt." So, what was Jesus' answer? He quoted the scriptures and said, "It is written, thou shalt not tempt the Lord thy God." He could refuse the temptation with the word of God.

The devil then came out with a third temptation. He said, "I'll make a deal with you. If you bow yourself down before me, I will give you political power over the whole world. You will become a skilled politician and have great political power. You will be a popular leader." Jesus answered, "Get thee behind me Satan: for it is written, 'Thou shalt worship the Lord thy God, and him only shalt thou serve.'" Then the devil became very frustrated and left him.

---

3 - *See:* Luke 4:1-13 and Matthew 4:1-11.

These are the three temptations. They stand for all the various temptations we have to refuse in our lives if we are on the path toward Christ consciousness. These are very instructive, these stories from the Bible. They give us strength to cope with the temptations of the anti-Christ. The specialty of the anti-Christ is this—we see it among students of Metapsychiatry: they start out very enthusiastic about what they are learning here, but after a while—a year, two years—gradually they start questioning, "Isn't there a better way? Do I have to become a Christly consciousness? Couldn't I have a little compromise here?" Indeed, they discover it works a little and then they become furious at the Christly value system and start a propaganda campaign refuting everything that smacks of Christliness.

Student: What is the meaning of them getting so angry?

Dr. Hora: They are being asked to give up too much. They get mad at the system and start discouraging other students from following the path and throw monkey wrenches into their path, trying to alienate them from committing themselves to the Christly way of life. When this happens, little problems begin to crop up in their own lives. There can be financial problems, business breakdowns, diseases, various forms of aches and pains…and they get deeper and deeper into suffering.

There is a story of a man named Job in the Bible.[4] Job was also a very Christly man, but gradually he became anti-Christ until he saw that he was destroying himself by trying to discourage his friends from continuing in their quest for enlightenment. Then, of course, he repented and was saved. It happens very often that after a while, students of Metapsychiatry start becoming hostile to other students and try to discourage them from progressing. It is a common experience, and if we understand that it is built into the nature of human existence, we will not get discouraged. We will know what is happening. We get over it and move toward ever more perfect

4 - The Book of Job: 1-41.

life in the "land of PAGL." These things do happen.

Student: In the beginning of the story, you were explaining the process, that the individual had understood something to a point, but then it goes wrong—some desire comes in.

Dr. Hora: One of our students, a very talented, very sincere young lady, has made a great deal of progress in studying Metapsychiatry. So much so that she is now in practice for herself and helping other people. Her husband started out with her, also studying, but he gradually began to compete with her and couldn't stand the fact that she was making progress. She was being transformed and blossoming and even economically prospering, whereas he was going downhill, constantly making remarks against Metapsychiatry. He tried to impede her studies, and became malicious. Fortunately, she kept prospering. She moved away and she is safe. He is going downhill in many areas of his life, and he doesn't want to see the problem and is courting disaster for himself through that anti-Christ behavior.

We are dealing with life itself in a nonreligious but existential way, and it is good to know that these things are inevitable but not necessary. It is not necessary if we can see through the machinations of the human mind that espouses the role of the anti-Christ.

Student: As we look at the world situation, it seems that the world's interest in being Christlike is ebbing very low right now.

Dr. Hora: No, you cannot say that. It has always been the same. The waves come and go and no one has succeeded yet in stopping the waves from moving, and that is how it is in life; but we can ride the waves. All you need is a plank of wood—a surfboard! (*Laughter*) It is the surfboard of understanding what the devil is. There is a saying: "What the devil is going on here?" This is called transcendence. We need to have dominion over the anti-Christ by getting acquainted with it. Not being afraid and not running away from it and not denying its presence. We deal with it to understand it.

Student: So what is it? Is it a denial? Is it jealousy? It's not a person.

Dr. Hora: Right. It is all those things: envy, jealousy, rivalry, malice — the "Four Horsemen"[5]—and a few other things too, such as temptations and ignorance. If you haven't learned to watch television with disinterest, you can get seduced into becoming involved with whatever goes on—politically, sexually, and economically. The television is a wonderful invention, but it is very dangerous. It is very dangerous if you don't know how to transcend the messages and see through them.

Student: If we say, "Nothing comes into experience uninvited,"[6] what would be the purpose of the anti-Christ?

Dr. Hora: It's a lesson. Without the anti-Christ, everything would be too easy, and we wouldn't even be interested. Problems keep us going; without them, nobody would come here, and I would have nothing to do. (*Laughter*)

Student: Is it meaningless to say there are more invalid thoughts than valid ones?

Dr. Hora: The computer has not been invented that would be able to deal with the number of invalid ideas. It is not a statistical issue; it is a subjective issue.

Student: With television, for example, it's difficult to find something of quality. There is a lot of trash out there. You could turn it off, I suppose—

Dr. Hora: We don't say, "Turn it off." We say, "Look at it with disinterest." You can look at all the television in the world, as long as you are not unduly interested in it. That way it doesn't hurt you.

Student: When it comes to interest and disinterest, when meditating, I get thoroughly distracted. Thought goes from here to there, every

---

5 - "The process of spiritual maturity entails outgrowing the galloping evils of 'the four horsemen.' The 'four horsemen' are: Envy, Jealousy, Rivalry, and Malice." *Beyond the Dream, Session No. 56.*

6 - The Seventh Principle of Metapsychiatry.

which way. I am meditating to try to understand some truth; then I ask myself, "Am I really interested in knowing this?"

Dr. Hora: That's a good question.

Student: The answer is, "No!" (*Laughter*) Then I ask myself, "What am I doing here, then?"

Dr. Hora: A very good question.

Student: I am at a total loss. Then I take out the Bible and get a quote, and at best I am intellectualizing. It is going nowhere.

Dr. Hora: That's about it. (*Laughing*)

Student: I'm feeling stuck.

Dr. Hora: What is the purpose of meditation?

Student: For me it seems to be to come to know and understand the truth of who I am and what my purpose is.

Dr. Hora: Millions of people are praying and meditating and going to church and joining religious groups, and then you ask them, "What is it that you are doing? What motivates you? What are you seeking?" They are seeking membership. Usually it's that they want to belong to something. Does Metapsychiatry have an answer to the question, "What's the purpose of meditation?" Is it good? Is it bad? Is it fashionable? Is it silly?

Student: I think, as the other student said, it's to come to know the Truth of Being.

Dr. Hora: Is that what he said? That's good! Once you know the Truth of Being, what will you do with it? (*Laughter*)

Student: All it does is contrast with what I am *not* doing. (*Laughter*) It just highlights how ineffective I am in meditating.

Dr. Hora: If it's any consolation, once there was a young man here, a student, who said, "In coming here and studying Metapsychiatry, I hope when I am finished, I will have sex with feelings attached to it." There are all kinds of fantasies connected with what we do. Another student, a lady, was buying gas for her car, and the attendant saw the book *Beyond the Dream,* and he started asking her questions, and he asked her, "What is it that you are reading?" She said, "I am studying to be a nicer person." Then the gas station attendant said to her, "Do you know what 'beyond the dream' means?" She said, "What does it mean?" He said, "'Beyond the dream' is Reality." She didn't know that, but *he* knew that! (*Laughter*) Then she asked *me* about "beyond the dream." Beyond the dream is another dream—until you run out of dreams, and then you enter the Universe of Mind.

Student: So we highlight erroneous motives. I still say I have the wrong motive. I know what the motive is. I have identified it as wrong. I am still going nowhere. I am still at the same point. Next time, I will still have a different wrong motive, but I'll still be at the same point.

Dr. Hora: Yes. What is the motive of the Christ?

Student: (*Hesitates and sighs.*)

Dr. Hora: You don't know?

Student: Well, I probably know. For the past couple of weeks I've been saying the answer to myself. What good does it do? I am still at the same point. I am just talking to myself.

Dr. Hora: Yes.

Student: Perhaps he is describing that he is at the stage of recognition but not at the stage of regret.

Dr. Hora: He seems to be regretting not getting anywhere.

Student: Regretting not getting anywhere is not the same as regretting the invalidity of the wrong motive.

Dr. Hora: You cannot win at that lottery. No matter how much you meditate, your number won't come up. (*Laughter*) What are we expecting to get out of these studies?

Student: Salvation.

Dr. Hora: Salvation. What is that?

Student: To come to know Reality. To see our true being.

Dr. Hora: So what? This student would say, "So what? What is the big deal in being Christlike?"

Student: The difference between being finite and being infinite?

Dr. Hora: How could that make a difference? How could you be infinite if you are sitting there in that chair?

Student: It's the consciousness that is infinite.

Dr. Hora: Do you *really* know this?

Student: You might say I'm working on it. (*Laughter*)

Dr. Hora: One answer we could say, and you could all apply it to yourselves, is the First Principle.[7] What's the big deal about the First Principle?

Student: It points you in the right direction.

Dr. Hora: Which is?

Student: You put first things first. You are more interested in the good of God than in getting something.

Dr. Hora: What can God do for you?

Student: I think if I understand right, you lose interest in "What I can get out of it?"—right? (*Laughter*)

Dr. Hora: Yes. However, it's perfectly legitimate to have a longing for spiritual blessedness. Everyone longs to be happy, secure, and

---

7 - The First Principle of Metapsychiatry: Thou shalt have no other interest before the good of God, which is spiritual blessedness.

good and loving— to be aware that God is constantly with us and blessing us, and we can see that "all things work together for good" (Romans 8:28). When we see this, suffering and worries diminish greatly. There is no fear. There is just peace, assurance, gratitude, and love. It's worthwhile. Don't you think so? It's even better than chocolate mocha chip ice cream! (*Laughter*)

2
Immunity From Adversity

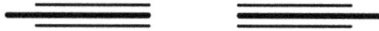

———— ————

Student: There seems to be a strange odor here, like rubber burning.

Dr. Hora: Yes, we are aware of it. There is nothing to be afraid of. When you go through hell you can smell the fire. (*Laughter*). What is hell?

Student: Life on earth.

Dr. Hora: Some people in California recently went through hell for two weeks. It was a hellish experience for them. One of our friends has a house near Malibu in a canyon, and the fires were raging around their house, and she sat up all night with the 91st Psalm and prayed and prayed and prayed. By the morning all the houses around there were burned down and her house was intact. She didn't even have to use the hose. The house wasn't touched by the fire. Now, in the Bible there is a story about Shadrach, Meshach, and Abednego. (Daniel 3) Do you know this story? Would you like to hear it?

Students: Yes.

Dr. Hora: Shadrach and Meshach and Abednego were Hebrew boys, and they were accused of worshipping a Jewish God, which was against the religion of the Persian Empire. It was at the time of Daniel. The king condemned them to be thrown into a "fiery furnace." They were thrown into this fire, and the king and others rushed to look. To his amazement he saw *four* individuals in the fire walking around comfortably. The description was that they all saw four figures, and "the form of the fourth is like the Son of

God." After a whole night in this fiery furnace, they were brought out intact, and the story goes that not even the smell of fire was on them. When you came in this evening there was the smell of fire; so, we are not yet as pure as these fellows.

(*Laughing*)

The meaning of this story is that these young men were so pure, so imbued with at-one-ment with God and Love, that nothing could touch them.

That brings up the question, how is it that some people are extremely vulnerable to fire, to strife, to seduction, to provocation? They are forever in conflict in with the world. They go from one trouble to another, involved in muggings, crimes, family discord, marital problems. There is just no end to it. They are constantly victimized by evil. On the one hand, the Bible presents us with such interesting stories of purity, innocence, and immunity. On the other hand, we have to see how people get victimized very quickly—hurting themselves and hurting their loved ones without even giving it a thought. Now, what lessons can we derive? We would all like to have good lives with love and harmony. We would like all life to prosper and to feel secure in this world. The Bible says it is possible. There are people who are not victims, who never get victimized. They are safe and live harmonious good lives. Then there also are many people who suffer. As a matter of fact, there are more who suffer than who don't. There is a line in the Bible: "Wide is the gate and broad is the way that leads to destruction, and many there be that go in…, and narrow is the way which leads to life, and few there be that find it." (Matthew 7:13-14) Here the Bible is teaching us what is needed for the good life.

Student: What is this narrow road?

Dr. Hora: It is the road of Christliness, of spiritual consciousness and spiritual uprightness.

Student: So, when the student you mentioned was praying the 91st Psalm, she was acknowledging the presence of God right there where she was.

Dr. Hora: Exactly. She was alone in the house with a little child, and the fires were raging all around. There was nothing she could do except pray. Fortunately, she had learned here about the 91st Psalm, and she leaned on its truth, and she was safe. Now, there were many people who prayed and they were not all saved. What is the difference?

Student: She was acknowledging that she is here for God, as opposed to God being here for her. Perhaps the others were praying for God to protect them from the fire. She was acknowledging the all-ness, the oneness, of God.

Dr. Hora: Yes, and beyond that, there was some purity in her soul from her previous studies. Her consciousness was not contaminated with the evils of the world. It is important to know how to pray and to be qualified to pray.

Student: What does that mean, "to be qualified?"

Dr. Hora: You have to be a sincere seeker of the Truth, not somebody who pays lip service to God, religion, this and that. You have to be a sincere seeker of the Truth so you can find conscious at-one-ment with the Truth.

Student: When you say "not contaminated by the world", do you mean by the "four horsemen?"[1]

Dr. Hora: Yes, right. What makes us vulnerable to "the adversary" or "the whisperer"? The devil has all kinds of names. A couple of weeks ago we spoke of "the anti-Christ." There are other names—"the adversary" or "the whisperer" or "the great whore." The Bible says, "Be sober, be vigilant for your adversary the devil,

---

1 - "The process of spiritual maturity entails outgrowing the galloping evils of 'the four horse-men.' The 'four horsemen' are: Envy, Jealousy, Rivalry, and Malice." *Beyond the Dream, Session No. 56, p.295.*

as a roaring lion, walketh about seeking whom he may devour." (1 Peter 5:8) So, there is an "adversary", a "devil", the "anti-Christ". There are no such persons. These names refer to the personification of human weaknesses and attachments to various ideas—like the "four horsemen". If we are envious, if we are jealous, if we are rivalrous, if we are malicious, then we are in danger of being invaded by this adversary, and we begin to be filled with all kinds of hostile or pornographic fantasies, or rivalrous, jealous, or even murderous ones. It is a very destructive condition. This adversary derives a strange kind of pleasure from hurting people or destroying whatever is good or worthwhile. There are people who have a passion to destroy anything that is pure and beautiful and true. They find all kinds of rationalizations.

These are the people who have been taken over by the adversary. What is the adversary? It is a mentality which is driven to prove that other people are wrong. No matter what they do, they have a great urge to prove that others are wrong. The adversary is constantly working to show that other people are wrong. When everybody is wrong, then you are king, but you are hurting yourself. The world is full of these thoughts, but the Bible teaches us that there is such a thing as immunity. We can be immune to the adversary. What is needed to be immune to the adversary? The Bible says we have to be sober; we have to be vigilant. What does that mean?

Student: "Sober" means not being distracted by pleasure seeking—

Dr. Hora: —including drugs or alcohol. Yes. So, you are sober. Your consciousness is not clouded. You can be intelligent about life, but you have to be vigilant. This means you have to be alert and be careful that you are not drunk or on any drugs or infatuated with something. When we are sober and vigilant, the adversary cannot overtake us, because we can see clearly. We are able to say, "I know what you are doing. I understand what you are after. I am in the service of 'the evil one' at this time. I am not guilty, but I am a victim of an invasion of evil ideas." The devil is like a roaring lion walking about seeking whom he may devour or destroy. Anyone who is invaded with false values like envy, jealousy, rivalry, and malice has an urge to destroy—to destroy even their loved ones.

I recently heard on the radio that a woman had cut off her husband's penis. Now what good would this do for her? She was married to this man, and she mutilated him for life! So irrational is this adversary! In a marriage it can easily happen—and in families. If they are not vigilant, they become adversaries—husbands and wives, and brothers and sisters. If they don't watch out, they become adversaries. They hate each other, and then they want to damage each other.

Student: Vigilance seems to imply a constant awareness of our thoughts. Normally when I am involved in something, it's usually later on that I realize I had been having wrong thoughts. Are you saying that if we are vigilant we can immediately correct it if we are having a bad thought?

Dr. Hora: That is correct. That is a mental discipline which we have to follow. We must be constantly alert not only to our own thoughts, but we must also be aware of the meaning of people's behavior towards us or towards others. If we understand, we are protected *and* we are not condemning them. We don't have to fight with them. We just have to see that it is a mental condition in which some people have the compulsion to be destructive of others. There are a variety of ways. If we are not vigilant, if we haven't learned to see meanings very clearly, we may become victimized without realizing it, and suddenly all kinds of things can start happening. We sit on a chair, and it collapses under us, or we are doing nothing and a picture falls off the wall. There are all kinds of things that can happen if there is an adversary mentality near us.

Student: How does one recognize what is happening? If we fail to be vigilant, then a day later we see we are in trouble.

Dr. Hora: The first sign is that we lose our joy. In the presence of an adversary, immediately we lose our joy. That is a warning signal.

Student: If you are joyless, you don't want to pray.

Dr. Hora: That happens if you don't understand the dynamic of non-verbal interaction between yourself and another. If you understand it, then you immediately turn to the First Principle[2] and silently acknowledge the truth of the good of God. This lifts you out of that mental climate which adversaries cast around themselves. There is protection in this. Those who don't know this or were not told about it become innocent victims. It can happen—sometimes in unexpected situations.

Student: How do we know if we are entering an adversarial environment or if we are part of it?

Dr. Hora: If you have lost your joy, you are already part of it. Jesus said, "My joy I leave to you; my joy no man taketh from you."[3] But if we get affected by an adversary and we lose our joy, we have already been conquered, and we are in trouble now. We can do two things—distance ourselves and run away from it or heal ourselves of this influence. We can silently remind ourselves that only God's thoughts constitute our being. We just shake off the influence of the adversary. This happens very often when somebody envies us or somebody competes with us or somebody is just obsessed with the idea of hate and judgmentalism and criticism. Some people are constantly criticizing, judging, and condemning people—in their families, outside their families, in church—everywhere. They are forever finding fault with everybody. You ask, "What is the way to be vigilant?" We are vigilant if we don't let anyone take our joy.

Student: Sometimes when we have to work with people on a project, they are extremely adversarial because they think they have to be

---

2 - The First Principle of Metapsychiatry: Thou shalt have no other interests before the good of God, which is spiritual blessedness.

3 - John 15:11; John 16:22.

right. They are very critical. They think no one can do as good a job as they can, and yet we have to participate with them on the project. No matter what we do, they always think it's wrong. I still find it hard to understand how we can really transcend that situation.

Dr. Hora: Right. (*Turning to another student*) Have *you* handled such a situation?

Student: It happens all the time. I just focus on the work that has to be done. It doesn't matter what the criticism is, because I'm not there to get rewards. I'm just there to get the job done.

Dr. Hora: Right. The worst thing is when people lose their joy, and they don't want to admit it. They tell themselves, "It is not true. I'm okay." (*Laughter*) Then they get worse, and then they develop a symptom of some kind—a backache, a neck ache, a headache. Today somebody called up and said, "I am full of ulcers, in my mouth, in my nose, on my body." Suddenly she broke out with all kinds of things. She didn't know how that happened. She didn't know what the meaning of it was. She thought she had a cold. These things can happen, and it is a great blessing to know that we need to be alert and aware and seek to understand that these are psychosomatic symptoms. They are just thoughts which we have allowed to enslave us. We don't blame anybody. We need to know that we must be more alert. The three Hebrew boys didn't blame anybody or complain. They were just immune. The Bible describes the protection beautifully: "When thou walkest through the fire, thou shalt not be burned; neither shall the flame kindle upon thee." (Isaiah 43:12)

Student: The human reaction is first to criticize and to blame and to be very judgmental. It is important to see that our first reaction is as a human person, but we can overcome the way the human person reacts and respond with understanding. Then we can be God-like and loving.

Dr. Hora: Yes, sure.

Student: When you lose your joy, you become very serious and lose your sense of humor. There goes cheerfulness. There goes joy.

Dr. Hora: Yes. That is what happens. Whenever you see a group of serious people, run! (*Laughter*) We have spoken many times before about the fact that seriousness is a killjoy.[4] We must guard against seriousness, and we have to learn to overcome. As the Bible puts it, "To him that overcometh will I give to eat of the tree of life, which is in the midst of the paradise of God." (Revelation 2:7) What does "the paradise" mean? Spiritual blessedness.

Student: It is possible to live in spiritual blessedness in spite of the world?

Dr. Hora: Absolutely. Sure. It is *necessary*. It is a holy act of asserting the truth of our freedom and the peace.

Student: Sometimes that holy act really elicits greater effort by the adversary. So, then what?

Dr. Hora: You have to win. It's a life or death struggle. Nobody has a right to take away our joy. "My joy I leave to you; my joy no man taketh from you." No one has the right to rob you of your joy. There are people who are suffering from depression, for weeks, months, and years, and they don't know where it comes from. They run to doctors, and the doctors have all kinds of chemical substances which uplift temporarily and then drop them even deeper into depression. There is no end to the struggle against depression, and that is their life. They are forever depressed, and they don't understand why. They ask, "Why am I depressed?" which is a futile question that doesn't give you any answers. Why is there an adversary? Why is there an anti-Christ? Why is there a devil? You cannot answer these questions. It just seems to be, that's all. We must learn to be aware. Nobody is to blame for that. We have a right to protect ourselves by refusing to get depressed. You see, the adversary wants you to be

---

4 - For example, see: Session 6, "Seriousness", in *Encounters with Wisdom, Book Three.*

depressed. He is working very hard, but if we refuse and we win, he will get mad, but then he will benefit from the experience.

Student: In the presence of the depressed individual, are we here to see the meaning of that for the individual?

Dr. Hora: We are here to see the meaning of the whole universe and everything in it from moment to moment, but we don't preach it. We respect people's right to be sick if they want to. Why would anybody want to be sick? That is a stupid question. We cannot ask, "Why?" There is a meaning if an adversary is depressed and angry. He also has a desire to contaminate other people and to spread his sickness.

Student: Do we have to go through hell and purgatory to get to the place where we can understand even a little bit?

Dr. Hora: Well, that is why you are here. This is hell and purgatory. (*Laughing*)

Student: I think that if we are able to understand some of the teaching, even though we are not *doing* anything, t it seems to come like a blessing.

Dr. Hora: Yes.

Student: But there are many others who are going through what seems like hell.

Dr. Hora: Yes.

Student: I wonder if it has anything to do with our evolving. I don't understand how it can happen.

Dr. Hora: How what can happen?

Student: How do we evolve from hell/purgatory to heavenly harmony—to spiritual blessedness?

Dr. Hora: We pray. We pray with utmost sincerity. The First Principle will get us out of hell into heaven. Shadrach, Meshach, and Abednego were lifted out of the fiery furnace. They were let loose. And none of their garments had even the smell of fire.

It is interesting—in the history of Christianity, early while Jesus was alive and shortly afterward, the favorite way of destroying people was through crucifixion, but later it became more sophisticated, and the method of destruction was fire. People were burned at a stake because they said a wrong word or they committed various acts seen as sinful. There was great fear spreading among the Christians, and nobody understood what the hell was going on. They didn't know to look for meanings. They only thought about "what should be and what should not be." Anybody who thinks in terms of "what should be and should not be" becomes a tyrannical madman who wants to destroy. Today we don't burn individual people anymore; we burn whole states and cities.

All kinds of evils of the world seem to be experienced throughout history, but nobody asks the question, "What is the *meaning* of this experience?" There is a strange kind of avoidance and reluctance to ask that question, not only here but everywhere. People don't even realize that they are avoiding asking that question.

Recently a young woman came to see me. She was diagnosed as having cancer, and she was very sad and very scared and facing a tragic future. She would have liked to know what to do and why this was happening to her. So, we spoke. She described in detail the interviews she had had with various doctors. I listened and I listened and I talked with her. After a while I said, "You spoke to me about what this doctor and that doctor said, and what they think." There had been debating about why and how, what should be done, and what is the best way to do it. And I said to her, "I haven't heard a single mention of God in your entire story. And there is another thing I didn't hear. You were exposed to Metapsychiatry a few years back, then you left. I haven't heard you mention the word 'meaning' or ask 'What is the *meaning* of this experience?'" Isn't that interesting? There she was in the throes of anxiety and facing a terrible future, and neither God nor meaning occurred in all the talk that was going on around her. Now, you could ask, "So what? Could that heal her cancer if she understood the meaning?"

Student: Could it?

Dr. Hora: Absolutely. God doesn't know about cancer. God only knows what Reality is. In Divine Reality there is no disease, and there is no "health"—good health or bad health. There is only the perfection of harmonious existence. If we can be lifted out of this mental prison in which we live with fear, things get healed, because our basic assumptions are altered and we have a different perception of life.

So, if somebody asks if Metapsychiatry can heal cancer, I say no, of course not. But the right understanding of the Truth of Being reveals the non-existence of disease, and then everything seems to be healed. When you realize, "2 and 2 is not 5, it is 4," it looks like a healing. It is not a healing. It is just the recognition of the truth of God's creation. What we are confronted with is always the need to come to know the Truth. Jesus said, "You shall know the truth and the truth shall make you free" (John 8:32)—not the doctor, not Metapsychiatry, not the Rabbi, not this or that, but the right understanding of the Truth of what really is.

Student: Doesn't that mean that the healing comes from understanding the "second intelligent question?"[5]

Dr. Hora: Yes. But it is not really a healing. It is the clarity of the Truth which we all need.

Student: It is a change in thought.

Dr. Hora: We cannot *do* it, but we seek to have the clarity of God's perfect universe. Metapsychiatry is not a healing method, it is a

---

5 - "In our pursuit of understanding Reality we have a method based on 'two intelligent questions.' In all our work in Metapsychiatry we ask two questions: (1) What is the meaning of what seems to be? and (2) What is what really is? With the aid of these two questions we are able to separate the real from the seeming, the good from the evil." *Beyond the Dream, Session No.1*, p.11.

matter of illumination of Reality. Whenever Reality is clearly seen, sickness is an impossibility, because there is no such thing. God never made sickness, either malignant or benign or trivial. God never made disasters. God never made any of it, and he doesn't even know about it. So here we are in fear and trembling and suffering and hating and envying, because we are ignorant.

There is a story of a Syrian army general who contracted leprosy.[6] In biblical times leprosy was a dreaded disease, somewhat like AIDS is today. It was a terrible thing for this Syrian army commander. So, he was advised to go to an old Jewish man named Elisha who lived by the river bank. It was believed that he could sometimes heal people. The Syrian general packed up his horses with all kinds of gifts and went to this Elisha, and as he was approaching the place where he lived, a servant came running to meet him and said, "Hold it! Don't come closer. Stop right there. What do you want of my master?" The people surrounding the general said, "We heard that you can heal people, and our general has this leprosy disease, and he came to ask you to heal him." Elisha said, "I cannot heal him, but I'll tell you what: there is the River Jordan, and if he goes and dunks himself into this river seven times, he will be healed." This infuriated the Syrian, who said, "What? I, a Syrian general, am to dunk myself into this Jewish river? This is the ultimate humiliation. I cannot do that." He turned around and was headed home. The people around him begged him to do it, because otherwise he would die. After a long discussion, he went and he did it, and he came out of this river completely healed. Now, he was so grateful, he wanted to pay for this healing, and Elisha refused to accept payment. He said, "I, a Jew, wouldn't defile myself with your money." (*Laughter*) This is my own version. (*Laughter*) There are situations where anyone can be proud.

Student: It was his pride that was healed.

---

6 - II Kings 5

Dr. Hora: The meaning of his leprosy was that he was a very arrogant and proud man, and Elisha knew that the way to help him was to humiliate him so that he would become humble rather than remain an arrogant, proud military man. And he did it. Elisha discerned the meaning at a distance. Sometimes we can see meanings very clearly—how people suffer from erroneous thoughts.

Student: Does it take humiliation to be healed?

Dr. Hora: You learn from a problem when your life depends on it. There is a Latin term *in extremis,* meaning "at the point of death." Elisha didn't heal him, God didn't have to heal him, but the change of outlook, more in keeping with the Truth, healed him.

Very often people complain that Metapsychiatry doesn't heal them. What do you expect? This is not a healing method. This is a transforming method. You transform your way of thinking to be in line with the truth of God, and it is the Truth which heals. I don't heal you. Metapsychiatry doesn't heal you. A book can't heal you. Nothing can heal you but realization of the Truth of Being. That is what we are learning to contemplate with utmost sincerity—the Truth of Being, day and night—all the time. We enter the gates of paradise with the help of the key to heaven, which is the First Principle of Metapsychiatry. The First Principle doesn't heal you. It opens the door to heaven, where you enter healthy. The moment you sincerely claim spiritual blessedness, you are happy, with no more problems.

There is *no* incurable disease, because in the Universe of Mind there is no disease, curable or incurable. People have a very hard time thinking this way. They seek a healing. It doesn't help to seek a healing. We seek the Truth. We seldom hear a Zen master talk about healing. They don't talk about it. Healings happen in those monasteries, but they don't talk about it because they don't want people to expect them to perform healing miracles.

Sometimes we can get so invaded by the adversary and provoked to such high degrees of rage and hatred that we can really hurt ourselves. Sometimes we carry around hatred in our hearts for years and we don't realize it, and then we get surprised that it is just pouring out of us for no good reason. It has been there, hidden for years.

Student: Doesn't it manifest itself in symptoms?

Dr. Hora: Yes, but you take a pill or go to the doctor, and the symptom is diagnosed as if it were something, but the hatred and anger are still there.

Student: In that case, are we keeping anger a secret from ourselves?

Dr. Hora: Yes. Sure. Sometimes we suspect that we have a lot of hidden anger and rage, and we would like to get rid of it, and we can't. We cannot willfully say, "I am not going to be angry," when we are actually angry. That is a problem.

Student: If the anger is from somebody else towards you, then what?

Dr. Hora: That is easier because we can be aware of that. Sometimes we can be very surprised at the hostile, angry attacks of some people against us.

Student: What is our protection?

Dr. Hora: We spoke about it. We refuse to give up our joy. We absolutely refuse to give up our joy. We stand fast, and the other guy gets fed up and gives up trying to provoke us. We pray for them. "Pray for them that despitefully use you and persecute you that you may be called the children of God. In thy presence is fullness of joy. At thy right hand are pleasures for evermore. For with thee is the fountain of life. In thy light do we see light."[7]

---

7 - Matthew 5:44; Psalm 16:11; Psalm 36:9.

3

Transcending Corruptibility

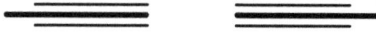

Student: What does the word "corruptible" mean in Corinthians? There's a passage that says something like "the corruption has put on incorruption."

Dr. Hora: "When this corruptible shall have put on incorruption, then shall it come to pass as it is written death is swallowed up in victory."[1] This is beautiful poetry, but what does it mean, right? What makes us corruptible? Does anyone think that he is corruptible?

Student: The desire to be liked. The desire to be loved.

Dr. Hora: Yes, right. The desire to be right and the desire to be admired and chocolate ice cream. (*Laughing*) We have a desire that people should think that we are right. All these things make us corruptible. There's a saying, "This judge is the best judge money can buy," right? (*Laughter*)

Student: What does "corruptible" mean? I don't really know what it means.

Dr. Hora: What does it mean to be venal? That is a stranger word than "corruptible." It means that we can be bought. When a judge can be bought, he is a venal judge. Here and there you run across somebody who will do anything for money. Does anyone think of himself as corruptible?

---

1 - So when this corruptible shall have put on incorruption, and this mortal shall have put on immortality, then shall be brought to pass the saying that is written, Death is swallowed up in victory. (I Corinthians 15:54)

Student: We could be corrupted by anything more interesting, either good or bad. Anything that takes our attention away from God.

Dr. Hora: How can anybody get corrupted?

Student: Like a child can say to a mother, "I will be good if you give me some candy."

Dr. Hora: This is not really corruption. This is just having a business sense. (*Laughter*) The integrity of the child is not damaged by getting candy for cleaning up his bedroom. But if somebody pressures you to lie and you give in and lie, then you have been pushed into a state of corruptibility. Suppose somebody insists that you agree with him and you say, "No, no, it isn't true," and finally the pressure is so strong and goes on for so long you finally say, "OK, I will give in and I will say what you want me to say."

Student: If it is so important to be liked or to have money, you are corruptible.

Dr. Hora: Yes. Very easily.

Student: And if someone is insisting that you agree with him, you might agree because you want that person to like you.

Dr. Hora: Yes. There was a famous astronomer, Galileo, who discovered that the Earth is revolving around the Sun, and at that point, nobody believed him, and of course the church came in and said, "You have to agree with the Pope and with all the religious clergy and say that you believe that the Earth is stationary and the Sun is revolving around the Earth. If you don't agree, we will burn you at the stake." There was tremendous pressure. After a while, he said, "OK, I agree." After he said that, there was a great relief in the audience in the church, and under his breath he said, "Nevertheless, it is still moving."

Student: He wasn't corruptible, then.

Dr. Hora: No, he yielded to political pressure—not for personal gain, only his life; not for money, not for fame, not for vanity, right? But he saw the situation—there was no hope that people would listen to what he had to say. He saved his life by yielding to the pressure.

Student: It sounds like it has to do with spiritual integrity.

Dr. Hora: Yes.

Student: Do we consciously allow ourselves to be corrupted, or does it just kind of happen and we have to be aware of becoming incorruptible? It seems like an important issue, because there are lots of distractions. Is the issue integrity?

Dr. Hora: Yes, that is the central issue—integrity. You see, Galileo preserved his integrity in spite of yielding to pressure. Suppose a guy comes to you behind your back and sticks a gun into your back and says, "Give me your money or I will kill you." You yield. You give him your money. Galileo's integrity was not violated. He just did what is prudent under such circumstances. So, this is not an issue of corruptibility. Corruptibility is when you are venal. When you do it for money, or for fame, or for sex. We have a Congress now in which there is a Senator who was so corruptible. There were dozens of women he seduced and abused. He was a very corrupt Senator. Who knows how many military secrets he may have given or sold for money? There are all kinds of ways that one can be corruptible, especially people in high places. People present you with gifts and all kinds of things. So that's the corruptibility.

Student: How do we understand what it says in the Bible, "Agree with thine adversary quickly whiles thou art in the way with him"? (Matthew 5:25)

Dr. Hora: It means, don't argue with your adversary. You don't have to win an argument. It doesn't make you corruptible when you see that someone is self-righteous and that it is very important to him to be right and for you to agree that you are wrong. So, you yield. You are not corruptible; you are prudent. If you "sell out," then you sell your integrity and hurt yourself. "If this corruptible puts on incorruption"—it is interesting—you "put it on." How do you put it on?

Student: By looking at what your values are.

Dr. Hora: And by looking at what the real issues are. People will argue and fight for ridiculous issues, especially in religious controversies.

Student: What does that have to do with death—that "death is swallowed up in victory"?

Dr. Hora: Good question. "Death is swallowed up in victory." It is a very serious business to be corruptible, because if your mode of being in the world is a corruptible mode, then a chain reaction follows that gets you further and further involved in inauthentic living. What is "inauthentic living"? You become a habitual liar, a deceiver. Someone who is not worthy of being respected…and you gradually destroy yourself. You can die from it. Some people deceive themselves that they are not corruptible, but they are.

Student: How would we know? It is easy to deceive ourselves.

Dr. Hora: It is easy, right? You can see you are getting in deeper and deeper; more and more situations arise when you have sold out in one way or another, and you develop all kinds of complications.

Student: "Sold out" in the sense of the Christly standard of living?

Dr. Hora: Yes, of course. In other words, you can die from being corruptible. Recently it was revealed on the news that several policemen were caught and confessed to drug dealing. They had become corrupt. They lost their integrity, and now they are losing their freedom, because for money they sold drugs and engaged in all kinds of things. It was devastating.

Student: How can we become incorruptible?

Dr. Hora: Incorruptibility—the Bible says you can put it on. What does it mean to "put it on"?

Student: You "put it on" in consciousness when you are turning to the Truth of Being, or even the First Principle, and you are focusing your attention. You are *putting on* a garb of spiritual clothing, and then if you are paying attention to it, you are "wearing" it.

Dr. Hora: Yes. It is a commitment. As you grow in your understanding of life, you begin to appreciate the freedom that Truth confers. It gives you freedom and peace and assurance. You appreciate it more than any amount of money, or personal or business connections and so forth. To "put it on" means you have committed yourself to live in an ethical way. So, you become incorruptible. This in turn protects you from various diseases and problems.

Every day those policemen would make thousands of dollars by stealing drugs from dealers and selling the drugs for their own profit. Drug dealing is going on in Central and South American countries and everywhere. The easy money that comes from it has corrupted the whole world. You find it in Asia, in Europe, here and everywhere. People are easily corrupted from drugs. Drugs, prostitution and crime—all these elements are signs of corruptibility.

Student: We can also appreciate that if we are corruptible, we are hurting ourselves. But many people behave ethically only because they are afraid of getting caught or punished.

*Dr. Hora***:** Who are you talking about?

Student: There are people who are honest because they think it is the right thing to do, but they don't really understand what we are talking about here, or they are afraid that if they are caught they will be punished.

Dr. Hora: Yes, this is true, and just because you haven't stolen anything lately doesn't mean that you are converted to the right way of life. That is why it is very important to understand that religion does not protect you from being corruptible. The religious argument is, "Be smart—don't do it because it is a sin, and by and by there will be no 'pie in the sky'."

Student: What does it mean that there is so much corruptibility on a global scale? Does it mean that we are losing interest in being spiritual, or does it mean something else?

Dr. Hora: It means that even though millions of people pray, read holy scriptures, listen to preaching and attend religious services, they don't really understand the existential implications of the holy teachings. They see them as just "old wives' tales." It is very sad that religion is no protection. Without understanding, you have no protection. St. Paul knew this when he said, "The good which I would I do not, but the evil which I would not, that I do." (Romans 7:19) Metapsychiatry says unless you understand the meaning of the Eleven Principles, you don't have a chance of living the right life.

It is particularly important to be aware of what we want, because that is where corruptibility is lurking. If we want something really badly, we become corruptible. Nothing must be more treasured than integrity. Integrity is very important. It is a lifesaver.

Student: Is it the same as honesty, or is it something more than that?

Dr. Hora: There are various degrees of honesty. Someone might say, "Well, I wouldn't commit a *major* crime—I am a nice person" or something like that. But, there are *no* degrees of integrity.

Student: What do you mean by integrity?

Dr. Hora: Integrity is from the Latin word *integer*, which means complete, flawless, undamaged, perfect. "Be ye therefore perfect even as your Father in heaven is perfect" (Matthew 5:48). That is integrity. Now, the question is, how can we become perfect? We are not gods, are we? Perfection is generally believed to be an impossibility. We often hear people say, "Nobody is perfect; nobody can be perfect," but Metapsychiatry says it is easy to be perfect. How do we become perfect?

Student: By being interested in it.

Dr. Hora: In what?

Student: In knowing what "perfect" is and what love is.

Dr. Hora: Knowing perfect love will get us to the point of existential perfection. If we learn to practice perfect love, we will be perfect. Is that so difficult? The fact is that very few people really know what perfect love is. There is a great blockage in the average human consciousness, because love is instantaneously thought of as a relationship. The moment you are conditioned to think of love as a relationship, you are lost. With such a view you cannot understand perfect love, because it is not a relationship. You know the song, (*Dr. Hora sings*) "I give to you and you give to me/True love"?[2] That's not it! (*Laughter*) In order to become perfect, Christ-like, we must understand and practice perfect love. Once you try it, you will like it, but very few people even think of it.

Student: When you say "practice perfect love," you mean we must realize it?

Dr. Hora: You cannot practice it until you realize it.

Student: Can we practice it even if we are alone? Does it mean we maintain a certain level of consciousness?

Dr. Hora: Yes. You practice it with a certain outlook on life. What is the First Principle of Metapsychiatry?

Student: "Thou shalt have no other interests before the good of God, which is spiritual blessedness."

[*The recording of the session ends here.*

The remaining segment of the class was not recorded.]

---

2 - "True Love", by Cole Porter. 1956.

4

Experience VS Realization

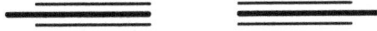

——— ———
——— ———

Student: My car was stolen last week. I went to get it a few blocks from here after group, and it was gone. I asked myself what the meaning was. I brushed it off, thinking it was the best thing that could have happened. I have insurance. In a way I don't mind, because the car was getting old. It's just as well it's gone. Why be concerned about the meaning?

Dr. Hora: You would like to have a new car. (*Laughter*)

Student: I didn't realize that until this car was stolen.

Dr. Hora: But now you realize it and now you are happy.

Student: Is that just "happy talk" that one says to oneself? Am I just making the best of a bad situation? I can talk myself into believing that it is not as bad as it seems and may be a blessing in disguise.

Student: When something like this happens, it does seem as though we feel that we should have some kind of a positive or negative reaction. He seems ambivalent, saying, "Maybe it's the best thing." I am thinking of the Zen master who said, "Is that so?"[1] These things

———————

1 - [This] story is about a very saintly Zen Master, living in a cave above the village. In the village there was a young girl who became pregnant. In her distress she made up a story that the Zen Master was the father of her child. When the child was born, the villagers became incensed and took the child and dumped him in the Master's lap, accusing him of being guilty of this shameful act. When the Master heard these accusations, he looked around and said, "Is that so?" and accepted the baby without protest. Years passed and the young woman had a change of heart; she confessed in the village that she had lied about the Zen Master, whereupon the villagers became incensed again, and a crowd of angry men and women came to the Zen Master, accusing him of keeping the child unlawfully for himself, whereupon the Zen Master, having listened to their accusations, said, "Is that so?" and

do seem to happen—babies come and babies get taken away, and the Zen master just says, "Is that so?"

Dr. Hora: Babies get taken away?

Student: Didn't he adopt a baby?

Dr. Hora: He didn't adopt it. He accepted it. That is an example of how wonderful it is when we are not attached to anything. This student is not attached to his old clunker. (*Laughter*) It is no big deal, especially in the city where you have public transportation.

Student: Maybe another issue it raises is that sometimes when things like that happen, we ask, "What is the meaning?" Every time something disturbing happens, it seems important to ask the meaning.

Dr. Hora: Yes, the good student asks the meaning.

Student: Let's say we drop a glass. Can we say, "The glass just fell"?

Dr. Hora: You can say that, but it is not so.

Student: Does every time something unusual happens have an important meaning?

Dr. Hora: It may not be important, but it does have a meaning. It is not always bad. Sometimes it is very good.

Student: Like in this instance?

Dr. Hora: Yes.

Student: It brings to mind the Bible story where Joseph gets kidnapped and sold into slavery and he gets elected Commissioner of Agriculture in Egypt. It seems that "all things work together for good—

Dr. Hora: —to them that love God." (Romans 8:28)

Student: We say, "Nothing comes into experience uninvited."[2] Can we therefore say that this experience of the car being stolen was invited?

returned the child. Beyond the Dream, Session No. 42
2 - Seventh Principle of Metapsychiatry

Dr. Hora: Not everything that happens to us is an *experience*. It is only an experience if we have a reaction. The enlightened man has a great advantage in that nothing comes into his experience—ever. Things come to his *attention*, but they don't come into his experience. What do you make of that? (*Turning to the student whose car was stolen*)

Student: Are you asking if the loss of the car came into my experience?

Dr. Hora: Yes.

Student: This is the second time this car was stolen. It was stolen three years ago.

Dr. Hora: You had to have it stolen again! (*Laughter*)

Student: Three years ago I was very upset because I was in rather tight financial circumstances, and buying a new car at that time would have been a financial strain. I was upset. This time, my finances are more comfortable. I was just a little inconvenienced.

Dr. Hora: It came to your attention but not into your experience. That is the ideal way to go.

Student: I don't know if this fits in here or not. You say that when we are enlightened nothing comes into experience. I was reading this past week about "rapture" and "ecstasy". To me those seem like feelings. Could you explain what they are?

Dr. Hora: Many people who are spiritually interested confuse things a lot. Some people on the spiritual path speak of experiencing "rapture" and "ecstasy." They are interested in sensations. They don't know the difference between *spiritual* joy, true happiness, and these carnal experiences. They use words like "rapture" and "ecstasy." Among many people who are studying spiritual truth, there is a secret fantasy that life will be more fun this way. They want to maximize the experience and have some kind of pleasure. They are still after pleasure, and when they talk like that, many listen to it. It is very fashionable to throw around spiritual words, but they really have not understood spiritual blessedness. It is quiet. No fireworks. No sparks are flying. Rapture and ecstasy have nothing to do with enlightenment. Enlightenment does not seek exaggerated sensations in life. It seeks peace, assurance, gratitude, love, freedom, wisdom, joy, beauty, harmony. That is what an enlightened individual appreciates. He is not looking for sensational experiences. You might hear someone say, "I had a big orgasm last night. I exploded!" Someone else says, "I ate caviar and it exploded in my mouth," right? They also believe that perhaps this is similar to what enlightenment is. These experiences are not like enlightenment. Most people are just seeking sensational experiences. We are not interested in experiences. We are interested in realizations.

The Bible describes this very beautifully when Elijah went looking for God. He went up on Mount Horeb. (I Kings 19:11-13) He was looking for God. As he was there hoping to see God, there was a tremendous earthquake. Everything shook, and the mountains were collapsing, and rocks were breaking up, and he looked, but God wasn't there. Then after a while there was a firestorm and God wasn't there. Then the Bible described that there was a hurricane and God wasn't there. Elijah was puzzled wondering where he was going to find God. The Bible described a "still small voice", and *that* is where God was. That is enlightenment. Elijah found God in the form of a still small voice. The voice of wisdom, the voice of love, the voice of beauty and harmony and peace. That is where God was all the time.

Ignorant students who don't have sufficient understanding, expect something fantastic to happen, and nothing happens. (*Laughing*)

Student: So, Elijah recognized God in that?

Dr. Hora: Well, I wasn't there. I am talking about what I read in the Bible.

Once a fellow here said, "After I have finished studying Metapsychiatry, I will have orgasms with feelings attached to them." That was his idea of enlightenment. (*Chuckling*)

Student: What is the definition of enlightenment?

Dr. Hora: Enlightenment is seeing the light. "Awake thou that sleepest, and arise from the dead, and Christ shall give thee light." (Ephesians 5:14) It is the light of enlightenment. When we see Reality in all its beauty and harmony—that peacefulness—that is enlightenment. When we understand all the shenanigans of unenlightened life, and the pronouncements of false prophets and gurus who teach all kinds of fantastic things, we are able to see that these experiences are not enlightenment. Happiness is quiet joy. That is happiness—quiet joy. How many people would get married if they knew that this is happiness? (*Laughter*)

Student: Would you say that quiet joy comes from being grateful for God's good?

Dr. Hora: Yes. All our foolish strivings, our "wants" and "not wants" disappear when we discover quiet joy.

Student: How does a "want" disappear?

Dr. Hora: It dies of neglect. (*Laughter*) We lose interest, but we cannot lose interest in *everything*, because then we would sink into a condition called apathy. Apathy is a form of depression where we have lost interest in everything that life has to offer. Apathy is a very bad condition of depression. It is also dangerous, because people do commit suicide in those situations. We have to be interested in the right values. Then we are not apathetic but enthusiastic. Enthusiasm is "being in God." We are enthusiastic for the Christly value system, looking always to be aware of God's presence and spiritual blessedness. So, our mantra is this: "God is spiritual blessedness." There is no other issue to be interested in. There is neither wanting nor not wanting. We are interested in the good of God, and that is nothing specific. You cannot sink your teeth into it, but you can be aware of the goodness which flows into our awareness from the Divine Mind. Therefore, our prayers, our interests, have to go in the direction of unspecified goodness. We cannot pray for a Rolls-Royce or something specific. God doesn't know about that. He is not interested in it. We cannot tell God what he should do for us, what he should give us or what he should not give us. All these prayers that concretize desires are futile. They are silly. God is not Santa Claus. We cannot tell or ask God anything, but we can constantly, silently remind ourselves that the only good that *really* is good is the good of God. This is spiritual blessedness. How do you grab hold of spiritual blessedness? You cannot measure it. You cannot weigh it. You cannot count it. You cannot do anything with it. You cannot bite it. You cannot possess it. You cannot have it, but you can be aware of it. All the good that is really good is always with you. That is why this is the only valid prayer. You can read all kinds of books that are teaching you how to pray, but they are usually interpersonal. "Have mercy on me, Jesus Christ, I am your friend. You are a friend of mine. You have lost blood for us." The tendency is to concretize. Most of the prayers you read about tell you how to pray concretely, and it makes no sense at all.

Prayer is just a conscious awareness of the good of God, which is spiritual blessedness, bliss consciousness. It is ephemeral. You cannot sink your teeth into it. If you pray those other prayers, you just get frustrated sooner or later. You hear pretty words in churches, imploring God and begging God, trying to get a handle on God, in millions of ways, and it is always in the direction of something three-dimensional—something concrete, something that should be or should not be.

When we pray, we don't say spiritual blessedness *should* be, right? Why can't we say that? Someone might say, "Hora said that spiritual blessedness is the best thing in life. Please, God, give me spiritual blessedness. Make it tangible so I can take it home," right? So, why can't we say this *should* be? We can't. We cannot ask for it. We cannot take it. We cannot reject it. We can do nothing with it. What kind of nonsense is this? The only thing we can do with it is to be sincerely interested in becoming aware of its presence and reality. That is the Alpha and Omega of prayer. Maybe if you knew how to speak in Greek, you could try that, but God doesn't speak Greek. God doesn't speak at all. God is. In the presence of God, everything is very clear and very good, and that is all there is.

Student: Maybe erroneous prayer has wide appeal because it is something you can wrap your mind around. Just what you described, real prayer is ephemeral, and when you make an effort to seek it, it seems very elusive.

Student: The Bible says to be still and listen when trying to understand the meaning of something. I try to listen, but my habit of trying to figure it out definitely interferes with listening. I am apparently listening for something concrete, and I know better, but I don't understand. Can you could help me? What is the listening?

Dr. Hora: When we *try* to listen, the problem is that we are expecting to hear some word or some noise, or some message in any language, and that is what Elijah described. He went to find God, and he was trying to listen for God, and he heard the sounds of an earthquake, a firestorm, and a hurricane. These things could be heard. God is not heard as a noise in any specific place. We are listening in the desire to become *aware* of a certain quality of life which is called "spiritual blessedness." When we are aware of that, if we are interested in that, that is what we will see and hear. All kinds of good things tend to happen around us and in us when we are sincerely interested in spiritual blessedness. That is how it works. God is not a chatterbox. It is of no use trying to get him to say anything. It is of no use for us to yell at him and demand things from him. It is a mysterious thing. For thousands of years people have tried to understand what God is and how man can be blessed by the knowledge of what God is. We are here to learn to be aware of what God is, because if we don't understand, life is just a tragic comedy of errors.

Student: Sometimes I find myself resisting the idea of just listening. It's difficult. I think I would rather do it or achieve it. When listening, I'm in a different mode.

Dr. Hora: Yes. We are not listening for sounds or for words or noises. We are not even listening to silence. There is a popular song: "The Sound of Silence." We don't even listen to the sound of silence. We listen to spiritual blessedness, which is an awareness of God's good, which fills the universe. If we can have contact with this spiritual blessedness, wonderful things begin to happen in us and around us. Zen meditation is very quiet. It is almost unendurable how quiet it is. In the West it is called "quietism." I think the Quakers have experimented with it, and many religious groups are experimenting with quiet meditation—listening to God. We have to learn this. We learn it if we understand that God is not a three-dimensional object.

Student: What about the intelligent ideas that seem to come with it? For instance, if we have lost something and then the right idea comes and we find it.

Dr. Hora: Sometimes it happens, yes. First you have to give up looking for it. Isn't that interesting?

Student: It is hard to explain. It's like a miracle.

Dr. Hora: Yes.

Student: Can we translate that to looking for God? We have to give up looking for God to find God?

Dr. Hora: Right.

Student: How would you explain that?

Dr. Hora: You don't look for God. You cannot look for God. Elijah was looking for God. He couldn't find God. He gave up looking for God, and suddenly he imagined he heard a still small voice, and that was God.

Student: He didn't have to climb that mountain. He could have stayed where he was. People travel all over the world looking for enlightenment, looking for the answers.

Dr. Hora: Right. They think they are religious and sincere.

Student: So often when I sit down to meditate or pray, I am looking for God, and I don't find him.

Dr. Hora: Yes. Usually what you are looking for is the *goodies* of God, and that is why it is so frustrating. When we are sincerely looking for God, we are looking for spiritual blessedness. This is not a person. This is not a thing. This is not liquid or solid. This is absolutely non-dimensional. Have you ever looked for something that is absolutely non-dimensional?

Student: What is an idea, then?

Dr. Hora: An idea can be valid or invalid.

Student: It can be imagined.

Dr. Hora: Right. It can be fantasized, but a valid idea—it just happens. We cannot make it happen.

Student: Is a valid idea spiritual blessedness?

D. Hora: Yes. Right. It is interesting that people complain about evil, but there is so much evil in everybody's life and experience. It is something that nobody wants, and yet there are all kinds of evil in the world. People are experiencing evil. It is easy to know about evil, because evil is dimensional. It can be felt, it can be imagined, it can be willed, and it can be accepted and rejected. Evil is a whole different order of experience. For most people it is a mystery—how can evil happen to people who are good and religious? How is it that religious people are experiencing evil?

There is a rabbi who wrote a book called *When Bad Things Happen to Good People*. He asked the question "How can bad things happen to good people?", and he found an answer. What did he say? He said God wasn't powerful enough to prevent even Hitler's Holocaust from happening. This indicates that this rabbi is an ignorant man. It doesn't help anybody to give this kind of explanation.

The vast majority of the world does not know the difference between what is real and what is dimensional. The tendency is to see life in terms of dimensionality and sensory experiences. You can be good, you can be intelligent, you can be religious, you can be educated, you can be everything the world says you should be, but if you don't understand God, you are completely helpless in face of evil, and that is the condition of the world. We have more policemen. We have more crimes. We have more accidents. We have more evil in the world—more and more, even though there are people who are very educated and they know a lot. They may even know the Bible.

Today I was listening to a preacher on television. He engages in a lot of politics. He was preaching for over an hour about the anti-Christ, but he didn't understand the anti-Christ. He was just quoting from the Bible about some nasty person who is against spiritual values. The anti-Christ is not a person. The idea that man is inherently evil and that it is almost impossible to redeem him is invalid. Everybody enjoys being evil more than being good. St. Paul said, "The good that I would I do not, but the evil which I would not, that I do." (Romans 7:19) There are some people who, whatever they touch turns into a disaster.

Student: Is evil just not being aware of the good of God?

Dr. Hora: Yes. Evil is believing in its own reality and power. Sometime in the past, years ago, I was in the company of a certain brilliant man for a while. I sort of enjoyed his company and was very glad to know him. After a while I began to notice unfortunate things were happening to me and to others who were associated with this fellow. The closer we were, the worse things were happening, and I didn't catch on soon enough. After a while I was in an automobile accident and was nearly killed. The whole car was smashed, and

I had to be pulled out of the car before I got destroyed. I asked myself, "How could this happen?" I never had accidents. I never had these things, but I suspected there was something working in my consciousness to bring about such a terrible accident.

It took me about six months or so to suddenly wake up to the realization that everything around this man was turning into a disaster for his family and his friends, which included me. I nearly died from his friendship! I was closer to being destroyed at that moment than I had ever been through the wars, etc., but his friendship resulted in my almost dying in this car accident.

Then I realized that everything this fellow was interested in and everybody who was a friend of his was running into problems. After a while I saw it very clearly. This fellow was really cherishing evil in his heart, and he enjoyed destroying people in an invisible, friendly way. I narrowly escaped being killed. He didn't know that he was doing this—that he was somehow suggesting to people to run into trouble in various ways. After I woke up, I could see that this poor fellow was an anti-Christ, and he didn't know it and nobody could tell him. I watched him for a few years, and indeed whatever he tackled in the business world and in friendships got destroyed. Everything around him, everybody around him was hurt or destroyed. There are such people who are obsessed with seeing others fail, and they don't know it.

Of course, this was a tremendous lesson to me, because after this I was able to feel safe in his presence. I could recognize that individuals such as this have an obsession about seeing others "go busted"—get into accidents, get sick, go broke in business, have all kinds of problems with their lives. They are devoted to evil, and that is the anti-Christ. There are people who are addicted to opposing the good of God. The moment you can perceive it, you don't fight against it, you just become friendly, quiet, and observe the life which is taking place around them. You cannot cure them, you cannot talk to them, you cannot say anything, but you can be on guard and you can pray for them. As Jesus said, "Love thine enemy, bless them that curse you, do good to them that hate you, and pray for them that despitefully use you and persecute you." (Matthew 5:44)

Student: How do we pray for an enemy?

Dr. Hora: Praying for them is acknowledging that they too are children of God. They too are here for God, even though they don't know it. If *you* don't know it, your friendship is a disaster. How many of you had friends where the friendship was a disaster? It can be a relative. It can be a stranger. It can be an enemy. But the important thing is not to have a *relationship*. Just observe it with compassion and pray—and be on guard. Do not expect anything good to come out of such a relationship. You are protected by constantly acknowledging that the good of God is spiritual blessedness. "No evil shall befall me and neither shall any plague come nigh my dwelling place."[3] People don't know what is hitting them or hurting them; but everything has a meaning, and if you are open and willing to consider the meaning, you will find out how to be safe in this world, more or less, depending on the degree of your spirituality.

Student: Evil does appear to have power.

Dr. Hora: Sure. Ignorance is no protection from evil. An ignorant individual befriends somebody who secretly enjoys proving that God is bad or evil. An ignorant individual who thinks this is a nice guy and a brilliant guy, enjoys his friendship and gets into trouble. He doesn't know what hit him.

Student: How can we understand this without making it personal? We tend to blame someone for their thoughts.

Dr. Hora: We must understand that *nobody* can be blamed. It is ignorance on his part, and it is ignorance on our part for not seeing it. We have spoken here about self-righteousness. There are people

---

3 - "There shall no evil befall thee, neither shall any plague come nigh thy dwelling." (Psalm 91:10)

who are obsessed with the desire to be right, and then there are people who are obsessed with the desire to prove that you are wrong, and then there are people who are obsessed with the desire to prove that there is no God. If we are spiritually minded, they will have the desire to prove that we are fools. We need to see that this is nothing. They have this problem, and they cannot really be blamed. We seek to be compassionate. Once we have discovered that because we have developed a relationship with such an individual, this problem is operating in our life.

We cannot blame any person, but there are these phenomena. Throughout history people have persecuted others—sometimes they even burned them at a stake because they thought that they had certain malicious inclinations. It is very dangerous to blame people, because then you yourself become a persecutor and then you are not a beneficial presence in the world. Ignorance is no protection. Vindictiveness is no protection. Judging is no protection. Condemnation is no protection, but discretion shall preserve you and understanding shall keep you.[4]

---

4 - "Discretion shall preserve thee, understanding shall keep thee: To deliver thee from the way of the evil man, from the man that speaketh forward things; Who leave the paths of uprightness, to walk in the way of darkness." (Proverbs 2:11-13)

5

Understanding Loneliness

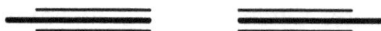

Student: I have an ongoing problem. When my husband's 6 year old daughter comes to visit I watch her being cruel or not loving. There is nothing I can do to change it. She is not my child; therefore she is not an extension of my consciousness.[5] There is nothing I can do to change it, and I just can't stand it! I can't do anything to help her. I can't do anything to help him. I am completely helpless. I hate being with the two of them, and yet she comes to visit every other weekend, and I am miserable when she is there. What do I do? Should I just leave the house for the weekend? I used to be able to cope with it. I can't cope with it anymore. You mentioned the last time we spoke that perhaps I have an interest in being important in their lives. How do I tolerate seeing her cruelty? She is not a loving child. There is nothing to love about her. She may be beautiful-looking, but she doesn't exhibit any qualities to love. She is not a lovely child.

Dr. Hora: And she *should* be loving. (*Laughter*)

Student: Is it all just "should" thinking?

Dr. Hora: That is all there is to it.

Student: If she is being cruel to her father or being nasty to him, showing no respect...

Dr. Hora: She doesn't like cauliflower.

---

5 - "In Metapsychiatry, we say that children are extensions of parental consciousness." *Marriage and Family Life: The Possibility of Frictionless Coexistence.* Section: "Family Values".

Student: She doesn't like anything.

Dr. Hora: You see, we are tormented not by people, but by our own "should" thoughts.

Student: You make it sound so easy.

Dr. Hora: Ain't it the truth? (*Laughter*) What a blessing it is to know this. There is so much suffering in the world, and we always look for what's wrong with other people. We think they are not the way they should be, and we want them to be the way we imagine they should be.

Student: So, *wanting* is also there.

Dr. Hora: Yes. They are practically synonymous: "wanting" and "shoulding." The interesting thing is that as long as we look at someone with this judgment, that they should change, they will never change; but when we give up having any demands whatsoever and give up judging and leave the whole problem in God's lap, then they can change.

I was watching a TV talk show—this one with mothers and daughters. There were several participants, but there was one particular mother. She was absolutely insane. (*Laughter*) She took on the whole audience, and there were about 100 people trying to tell her that she was wrong about tyrannizing her daughter—how she should be and how she shouldn't be. Nobody could get to first base with her. She had an answer for everybody. Every individual in that place was frustrated, including the leader of the talk show. No matter what anybody said, she always had a counter answer. At one point she turned to her daughter, who was 21 years old, and said, "I am your mother. I am telling you how you should be!" The daughter was arguing with her because she had already become like her mother, and there was endless argumentation. Everybody was frustrated. This woman was so vociferous in defending her position about child-rearing that nobody could get through to her. Everybody was terribly upset. It was a noisy kind of talk show.

When self-righteousness takes on such intensity, we are dealing with insanity. This is a psychotic degeneration of simple self-righteousness, which is not a rarity. People usually want to be right, and win the argument. But when it takes on such proportion, we are dealing with an insane individual, and any kind of attempt at helping her to see anything from a different perspective just provokes more violent defensiveness and self-justification and self-righteousness, and it doesn't help. It cannot be altered through discussion. It is absolute nonsense to try to convince anybody that he is perhaps mistaken or that his point of view is not valid. You cannot do that. You have to surrender your "shoulds" and allow people to think what they want. You don't have to obey them, but you don't try to convince a self-righteous individual that he is wrong. You cannot. It's an impossibility.

Student: Aren't people picked for these talk shows because they will be controversial?

Dr. Hora: Well, it's not difficult to find someone who is self-righteous. (*Laughter*) The whole audience became self-righteous, telling the mother that she shouldn't be so tyrannical and dictatorial to her daughter. Then the daughter piped up…

Student: This is what people enjoy watching. This is what the producers of the show like to promote.

Dr. Hora: This went too far. Everybody was upset. They had a very unpleasant experience.

Student: If our student here were to turn away from what she is seeing with the little girl, would the healing come in a way similar to when you lose something and you stop looking for it and then you find it?

Dr. Hora: Yes, exactly. Have you ever experienced this? If you lose something, don't try to look for it, right? You just acknowledge that Divine Mind, which is all-knowing, everywhere present, knows where it is and will reveal it to you eventually, when you are not looking. If you are looking, you are self-righteous, and you won't find it. You just remembered the story about the screw assembly in the forest. Many people remember that story[6]. (*Laughter*)

So, if you have a little girl who has already developed her own resistance and self-righteousness, leave it alone. Let it be. Don't get involved. Just be prayerful. The Bible tells us to pray for those who despitefully use you and persecute you and resist you.[7] It is a great blessing to understand this, because people who don't understand get involved in banging their heads against a brick wall.

You see this? (*pointing to a scar on his forehead*) That happened to me some years ago. I was talking with a self-righteous individual, and it was like banging my head against a wall. I tried to convince her that she was mistaken. Nothing—I couldn't get through to her! (*Laughter*) I got upset and I said to her, "Talking to you is like banging my head into a brick wall." Sure enough, the next day… (*Laughter*) Don't do it! (*Laughing*)

Student: The other element is, I watch the father, and he suffers.

Dr. Hora: He has a right to suffer, and you cannot help him. You can set an example of a gracious lady who is letting people be. That would be helpful, right?

Student: "Letting be." Could you explain that, Dr. Hora?

---

6 - "…I dropped an assembly of two little screws [in the forest] which fell apart and disappeared among the leaves. I started kicking the leaves around, but it… occurred to me that the harder I searched, the more impossible it would be to find the screws. So, I decided not to look for it. God is all-seeing Mind; this Mind can see where those screws are…. As I became more and more quiet, my eyes were drawn to a spot about two feet away from me and there, among the leaves, I saw a little metal object glistening. I picked it up. It was part of the screw assembly. …I said, "Thank you God. If you could show me this one, you can also show me the remaining part because you are the all-seeing Mind and I am part of you." … I was standing there quietly…. My eye was drawn…about two feet away from the first spot, and again, among the leaves, I found the second part." Dialogues in Metapsychiatry, Dialogue No. 29: "Ambition".

7 - "But I say unto you, Love your enemies, bless them that curse you, do good to them that hate you, and pray for them which despitefully use you, and persecute you…" Matthew 5:44

Dr. Hora: "Letting be" is love and respect for someone's right to be wrong.

Student: Is that different from passively putting up with it, being patient?

Dr. Hora: That is not letting be. That is called "agonizing."

Student: In order to let be, we can't want something from the other. Wanting is what really makes us vulnerable to this misbehavior. We want something. We want good behavior.

Dr. Hora: We want agreement. We want people to see things the way we see them, and we want people to be nice. We have no right. You have to learn a very important lesson, which is called "letting be."

Student: If you see that someone is inviting abuse, there is still nothing that can be done.

Dr. Hora: Oh, yes. If someone is inviting abuse, you refuse to give it to him, and then he will be unhappy. Right? Somebody demands that you agree with them. What will you do? You try to explain to him, "You want me to agree with you." He says, "No, no, I just want you to see the way I see the situation." So, then you could lie, but then he is smart enough to know that you are lying and he's not happy about it. Debating doesn't lead to a resolution. There is only one thing that leads to resolution: silence—sympathetic silence, which is compassion. Discretion shall preserve you[8], compassion shall heal you, but secretiveness and secret hating, secret insisting and secret cursing and secret willfulness, can kill you.

Student: So just putting up with it is another form of secretiveness.

Dr. Hora: Right, exactly. We must learn to let go and let God. God is right there. He is waiting. He is waiting for us to let go.

Once I saw a child in the supermarket standing in the carriage with the groceries, and he was screaming his head off nonstop, and the

---

8 - "Discretion shall preserve thee, understanding shall keep thee…" (*Proverbs 2:11*)

parents were so embarrassed. They did everything possible to make him stop, and the harder they tried to shut him up, the harder he was screaming. People were running out of the store. (*Laughter*)

Student: Funny, the irony of it. I took the bus here, and when I got on the bus, there was a toddler sitting on the front seat, greeting everybody hello, smiling, joyful, happy. I said to myself, "Now, *that* is a child."

Dr. Hora: That's how she *should* be. (*Laughter*)

Student: Dr. Hora, you said before that you pray about it. Would we be directing our thoughts toward the child? Would it be more like perfect love—projecting it to the child? How would you pray in such a situation?

Dr. Hora: What is the difference between prayer and silent manipulation? That is what religious hypocrisy is—silent or ritual manipulation. In this kind of prayer, there is self and other. Whenever our prayer contains the structure of self and other, immediately it is void, because in the realm of Divine Reality there is no dualism. There is no self and other. We cannot pray for another. Prayer is the acknowledgment and the sincere contemplation of the Truth of Being. There is no God *and* man, right? What is there? There is God *as* man. Is this clear? God as man, and there is no "two." Effective prayer must be in the realm of the nondual. Divine Reality is nondual. Hear, O Israel, our God is one God.[9] There is no "two."

Student: Suppose I walk into this situation and the child is misbehaving. What do I need to realize?

Dr. Hora: The best thing is to pick yourself up and run out. (*Laughter*) This is a karate principle. Have you heard about that? The first principle in karate is, if somebody is provoking you, you run. (*Laughter*) That is the wisdom of karate, of martial arts —the art of running away. The Zen master says, "In the realm of the real, there is neither self nor other; there is only that which really is." To many

---

9 - "Hear, O Israel: The Lord our God is one Lord." Deuteronomy 6:4

people this is a koan, a mystery. "How is that? What do you mean? You are talking in riddles." There is only that which really is. What does it say? The enlightened prayer is a conscious understanding of Reality. In Reality, there is no self and other. There is only Reality— all-encompassing, infinite Love-Intelligence—and if we would like to pray, then we focus our sincere attention on the task of becoming aware of what really is. In "what really is," there ain't nothin' else, and the more clearly we can understand and cherish the Truth of Being, the more clearly we can always bring this knowledge to bear in whatever situation is claiming our attention. You see, the world has three ways of claiming our attention. What are the three ways? Seduction, provocation, and intimidation. If we know this, there is no problem, and things have a chance to become harmonious, because Reality is harmonious and intelligent and benevolent. The more we understand Reality, the more effective our prayers are. There is no "he" and "she." There is no such thing. Consider the fact that all the psychologists in the whole world are forever trying to improve relationships between people—they are working and teaching and trying to help others develop good relationships between "self and others." This is not possible. Contrary to general belief, you cannot have a good relationship with *anybody*. Not even with Jesus Christ could you have a good relationship. There is no such thing.

Student: So, understanding God *as* man eliminates our sense of personhood.

Dr. Hora: It eliminates the dualistic misapprehension about life.

Student: I can understand what you have been saying when I am by myself, and I really am aware of Reality to a certain degree; but then I find when I am in the midst of a situation where I am being provoked, I can't find the same awareness that I could when I was by myself. Does that mean that I really didn't understand it?

Dr. Hora: You need more sessions here. (*Laughter*) Reality is not changing—it is unalterably nondual. People tend to pressure each other. Regardless of what anybody says or thinks or tries to elicit from you, if you respond to the pressure, you slide into dualism.

Student: Often the people we are with are not interested in seeking the Truth.

Dr. Hora: "Stand fast in the liberty wherewith Christ has made us free, and be not entangled again with the yoke of bondage," of thinking of yourselves as separate persons—as self and other. (Galatians 5:1)

If you are lonely and find yourself thinking, *I am all alone,* where are you? In "Never-Never Land." It is not possible for God-as-man to be alone. "I and my Father are one." (John 10:30) Are there two, or is there one? Do I choose dualism, or a nondual realization that there is no such thing as being alone? I wish I understood that. For a long time I was struggling with this and still do, because it is hard to realize that we are always an inextricable aspect of God and we can never be alone.

Student: I wonder what it is that makes us think that we are alone? What is that thought?

Dr. Hora: It is a habit of judging by appearances.

Student: Seeing something else?

Dr. Hora: It is always the idea that there is self and other. There is a lot of suffering on the basis of this assumption that if there isn't somebody else nearby, then we are alone. That is a great problem to outgrow. God is never absent.

Student: What do you mean, "God is never absent?" What is the definition of God? What is it we seek to realize that we are not absent from?

Dr. Hora: God is infinite presence. Can you absent yourself from infinite presence?

Student: No, I guess not. Somehow we have to realize this in consciousness—non-dimensionally. That's where it gets difficult. As you say, we can't sink our teeth into it, so we have this sense of emptiness.

Dr. Hora: Yes. Jesus said, "I am never alone. My Father is always with me."

Student: So, is loneliness the absence of the awareness of God's presence?

Dr. Hora: Right, surely. Yes.

Student: So, we can be with people and yet feel very alone.

Dr. Hora: Yes, of course. On the other hand, you can be isolated and still *not* feel lonely.

Student: Everything is all right.

Dr. Hora: Yes.

Student: There seems to be something about being engaged in useful activity, because even when we are by ourselves, and ideas are flowing and there is creativity, there is no thought of loneliness.

Dr. Hora: Yes.

*Student***:** But sometimes we could even be meditating and somehow be lonely.

Dr. Hora: Yes. This is a very important stage on the path towards enlightenment, the overcoming of the sense of loneliness and isolation. Of course, this is the problem with grief. When we lose a loved one, we go through the excruciating pain of loneliness. Unless we are helped to understand the inseparability of God from all creation, we are never really healed of grief. We just replace it with other dualistic concerns. When we have a sense of loss, we see ourselves as "losers" until we understand that nobody is a loser.

Student: It seems that when I am lonely and thinking in terms of interaction, my mind starts to race with interactive solutions, like wondering, "Who can I get to do this?" or "Who can I get to like me?" or some other interactive thought. It is totally useless.

Dr. Hora: Yes. Sometimes you buy a dog and heal yourself of your loneliness; but it is never quite enough. Then you buy another dog. Pretty soon you have many dogs, and then you don't have to deal with people anymore.

Student: I relate to what she said about being alone to meditate and realize the Truth and PAGL. I find that too. It is when others appear that it becomes troublesome and all the good disappears and I become interactive. I am not ready to be with others. It seems it is easier to understand what we have been studying when I am alone. Sometimes when I am with friends I become uncomfortable and can't wait to get away. An hour with someone might be enough, and I would like to be able to leave.

Dr. Hora: That is how we become hermits. What is a hermit? Is a hermit an enlightened man who has no need for companionship?

Student: I don't think so.

Student: Last week, Dr. Hora, you said that we need to be "cautiously friendly." Doesn't that border on being a hermit? It seems close to it.

Dr. Hora: A hermit rejects people. To be alone is a statement of dualism.

Student: A lot of times with people—not that I hate people—it's that we don't have the same values. Where I live, there is a pool. There is a lot of socializing that goes on. People usually invite me over, and I can put up with it for half an hour. After that, the discussion is just not what I am interested in. I can't get that involved in it, and I'd just as soon bow out.

Dr. Hora: It is a serious problem for everybody to wrestle with, because to be with people is dualistic, and to be without people is also dualistic.

Student: Jesus used to go off by himself. He would get up early and leave, but he always came back. Perhaps we have to do that, too. Perhaps reading or meditating, then being with friends, then time away, then going back into the fray—going back and forth.

Dr. Hora: Jesus struggled with the problem of abandonment, rejection, loneliness, and resentfulness. He struggled. Afterward, he came up with the statement "I and my Father are one." At that point, he realized that there is no solution to this issue of loneliness or coping with loneliness without fear, a sense of missing something. We don't know how much time he spent trying to realize at-one-ment. Everybody has to struggle with this problem, and everybody finds temporary solutions, like having pets. We struggle until such time we understand *God as man*. We are what God is. There is an inseparable at-one-ment with God. Reality is nondual. I have never known anybody who has found peace on the wrong basis. People find peace temporarily, like for instance if you have good food. If you are a glutton, you don't need anybody. You think that you've got it made until something happens. But Jesus came to the ideal solution. I don't know at what point in his career he was able to say, "I am in the Father and the Father is in me. It is the Father who dwelleth in me. He doeth the works."[10] I think at that point, he must have understood this great problem.

Student: I was thinking it is symbolic that at the end of his life, when he was going to be crucified, he wanted the disciples to stay awake with him for their support.

Dr. Hora: Right! He complained because they fell asleep and left him alone. This is not like an enlightened man, but he was forgiving:

---

10 - "Believest thou not that I am in the Father, and the Father in me? The words that I speak unto you I speak not of myself: but the Father that dwelleth in me, he doeth the works." (John 14:10)

"OK, go back to sleep; I will endure this loneliness and the pain of it." We have to struggle the same way.

Student: We endure the loneliness. Is the meaning of that that we don't know the inseparability, so we will always be lonely one way or another until we know that?

Dr. Hora: Until we understand at-one-ment. Yes.

Student: As you said earlier, unless we understand this we get only temporary relief from the sense of loneliness.

Dr. Hora: There is a story about a Jewish rabbi who felt very lonely, so to console himself he went to the deli. He goes over to the deli counter and, pointing, says, "Give me a half a pound of that pastrami." The man behind the counter says, "This is not pastrami—this is ham," (*Laughter*) and the rabbi says, "Who asked you?" (*Laughter*) He was trying not to be lonely.

Student: I seem to get preoccupied with the "sea of mental garbage" and all the interactive thoughts. Does this dull the loneliness? Does it distract me from seeing Reality?

Dr. Hora: Everybody who is not totally enlightened will feel lonely and miserable without companionship. That is why there is a constant quest for friends, for family life, for belonging in groups. We always want some arrangement whereby we could be free of the pain of loneliness.

Student: So those things are just escapes, then?

Dr. Hora: Temporary solutions that are mostly unsatisfactory.

Student: Without breaking through that, enlightenment wouldn't be possible.

Dr. Hora: Right. I knew a psychotherapist who was a Zen trainee. Karl Friedrich von Dürckheim—he lived in Germany. He devised a treatment method where he required his patients to spend certain nights once in a while in a cemetery, all alone. He sent them to the cemetery. He told them, "You have to be there all night. Don't come back until the morning." It was very radical.

Student: What was the idea behind that?

Dr. Hora: To experience the fear of loneliness. The idea is connected with dying or being dead. What do you do in the grave? It must be very lonely there, right? So, his patients were obligated to spend certain nights in the local cemetery. It is spooky, right?

Student: It is sobering.

Dr. Hora: Unless you take a bottle of whiskey. (*Laughter*) That is also a temporary solution, mostly unsatisfactory. Maybe addictions have something to do with this, because if you are taking some drug or alcohol, you solve the problem temporarily. You don't have to be fearful and uncomfortable with loneliness. You just get drunk, or the drug alters your consciousness, and you don't have to specu- late about the idea that you are lonely. You are lonely, but you are drowsy.

Student: Is the meaning of the fear of loneliness the fear of death?

Dr. Hora: Yes, of course. If you were dead, you would have it solved. It is not death that is the problem. Dying is the problem—the fear of dying —and therapy. Medical science has contributed now to the fear of dying, by introducing therapy.

Student: What do you mean, "the fear of dying is the problem, not death"?

Dr. Hora: Once you are dead, you have graduated.

Student: You mean the fear of the event—when it will come upon us? And the meaning of that is fear of extinction?

Dr. Hora: That is just another word. It is the idea of loneliness. We think of dying as going to a situation of eternal loneliness. That is nonsense.

Loneliness is one of the unpleasant experiences everybody has to wrestle with and find a solution to. There is only one right solution, and Jesus expressed it in words. Not even the Zen masters, I think, deal with the problem of loneliness, do they?

Student: Maybe they go out for a drink. (*Laughter*)

Dr. Hora: But it is not the right solution. If we are sincerely seeking to know Reality, to know the Truth of what is, we have to come to the point where the statement "I and my Father are one" makes a lot of sense to us.

Student: What do you mean about medical science introducing therapy and increasing the fear of dying? I am not sure what you mean by that.

Dr. Hora: Nowadays there are so many people who are suffering from medical malpractice that many are afraid even to consult doctors. So, you cannot get sick, and you cannot get treatment. There is not only a fear of sickness, but a fear of the therapeutic treatments. It is a terrible situation. Before the therapies were developed, there was only fear of sickness, and people coped with the fear of sickness through family life and human affection; but now, with medicine, scientific medical practice, we can be afraid of that, too.

Student: Some life! (*Laughter*)

Dr. Hora: As they say in some circles—life sucks.

Student: If you want to be correct, you say, it is a "challenge". (*Laughter*)

Dr. Hora: Ah, politically correct.

Student: Another coping mechanism for loneliness is just *doing*. Someone mentioned earlier being useful; but there is a lot of "doing" that is not very useful. It is just busyness in order not to feel alone. It can be just another distraction.

Dr. Hora: There are millions of solutions that people devise for themselves to make life bearable.

Student: How can we tell? It may seem that it is needed, but maybe not. How can we tell what is useful and what is not?

Dr. Hora: Usefulness is part of our dedication to God. It is almost a religious activity. When Jesus became enlightened, he didn't have to do anything anymore. He just realized , "I am in the Father and the Father is in me" and there was spiritual blessedness. Sometimes we can find a lot of comfort by reminding ourselves of the First Principle. [11] There is a great deal of comfort to be found in it, and also strangely enough, good things have a tendency to happen if we stay with that First Principle. It is a great gift of God to know this principle and to stay with it—like a mantra. You know what a mantra is? The Oriental sages devised certain phrases or words, like "Om," that are repeated ceaselessly— silently or out loud. It is probably a way to maintain an awareness of Reality, because if you are not in touch with Reality, you start fantasizing, start evolving images and even activities that will not really give you what you need, and you don't find peace. It is not helpful. So, a mantra is probably more helpful than any kind of diversion and certainly less harmful than drugs and alcohol.

---

11 - The First Principle of Metapsychiatry: "Thou shalt have no other interests before the good of God, which is spiritual blessedness."

6

Concentrating VS Paying Attention

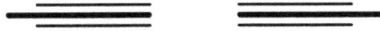

Student: I have a "how-to" question. How do I listen and try to understand what is being said, if what I'm really thinking about is what people think of me? I have to concentrate on what is being said but at the same time I am wondering if people think I'm stupid. Is it possible to sit here and rise above thoughts that people might think I'm stupid? (*Laughter*)

Dr. Hora: (*Laughing*) It is hard.

Student: But is it possible?

Dr. Hora: Now if we would like to show that we are intelligent, we have to understand the difference between concentrating and paying attention. Does anyone understand the difference?

Student: In concentrating we think that personal mind is doing something, whereas intelligence is spontaneous with thoughts obtaining in consciousness.

Dr. Hora: Yes. Well, this is true. Could you explain this in such a way that all of us who are stupid could understand?

Student: Well, I recall when I had difficulty going to school you always said to me that if I could just learn to listen to understand, the understanding would make the difference. I remember focusing on what it means to understand. Any time I tried I realized I was trying to memorize the information and this made absolutely no impact on my life at all. The only way that anything was internalized was when I just somehow relaxed in the idea that God will provide the understanding. All I had to do was shut up and listen. (Laughter) That thought helped me throughout school because I wasn't allowed to be "intelligent." I wasn't allowed to be "smart." I couldn't do any of those things, so I had to give up that notion and just learn to listen.

Dr. Hora: Yes.

Student: I guess it would be helpful to understand what "understanding" is and what the dynamics of that is. It is certainly not a personal effort.

Dr. Hora: Yes, so now we have expanded on the problem. Now we not only have the issues of concentration and of paying attention, but also of understanding.

Student: Isn't it all related? I mean, whenever it is a personal effort it doesn't work.

Dr. Hora: Right.

Student: It would seem that concentrating is required when we are distracted by other things. When our interest is really elsewhere, it is necessary to concentrate in order to narrow the attention, whereas "paying attention" seems like more of a natural thing that occurs when we are genuinely interested in something and have that involvement which interest imparts.

Dr. Hora: Could you explain it better to those of us who are stupid?

Student: When concentrating, one is involved in an effort where there is not a genuine interest in the subject. When we are distracted by other concerns, like the fear of appearing stupid, we have to then focus our attention in such a way that we call "concentration," which is a personal effort; whereas paying attention comes naturally when we are interested in something—when that is our primary concern.

Dr. Hora: In one of the books on Metapsychiatry, there is a question posed by the author. (*Laughter*) The question is, "What is the payment when we are paying attention?"[12]

Student: We give up self-concern.

Dr. Hora: Did you hear what she said? We give up self-concern. What is happening when we give up self-concern? Suppose we are preoccupied in a self-concerned way with our new hairdo? Certainly, if we are preoccupied with our hairdo, we cannot pay attention, yes? We are concentrating on what kind of a hairdo we have or want. There are a million things we can concentrate upon, and the more we are in the habit of concentrating, the more danger there is that we become computer consultants. When we work with computers, we have to concentrate. Isn't that the truth? Sometimes when we run into a snag and if we try to figure it out, we concentrate, and it doesn't work, right? This difference between concentrating and paying attention is extremely important. It is a well-kept secret and not many people know about this. Fortunately, many people spontaneously know how to pay attention. What is required to pay attention?

Student: Interest.

Dr. Hora: Interest, right. How do we do the "interest" bit?

Student: We do it when we realize the value of something. When we realize the value of it, we are automatically interested.

Dr. Hora: Yes. Do you remember the incident we have talked about, of the screw assembly which got lost in the forest floor?[13] As long as we wanted to find it we were concentrating on looking for it and we couldn't find it. When we gave up looking for it, then we found it.

There are many people who are very anxious about using their heads. You have all kinds of sayings like, "Use your head, stupid!" (Laugh-

---

12 - *In Quest of Wholeness*, p. 9.

13 - *Dialogues in Metapsychiatry*, Dialogue No. 29: "Ambition", p.155.

ing) At IBM they have a slogan for employees: "THINK." When you are involved with thinking, you cannot pay attention. You just keep thinking and you never get anywhere. Rodin's statue of "The Thinker" expresses this dilemma very clearly. He is *thinking*. He is so involved with himself that his body is contorted [with his right elbow resting on his left knee]. If we would like to be intelligent, effortless, effective and efficient, we have to know the difference between concentrating and paying attention.

Student: When I listen to the tapes of your group sessions, most of the time I am concentrating to absorb it all because I realize that there is value in what you're saying. I want to be able to take it all in. This past weekend I was very troubled and listened to a tape in which a student asked a question, "Don't we need to be loved? Isn't that a legitimate need?" You answered, "No. God is love and we are what God is." I found that I was healed. I became aware of PAGL and my whole consciousness changed. Everything that had been troubling me disappeared. It was gone! I went on with my chores in a whole new state of consciousness. This was very different from the way I usually listen to the tapes. This was a healing that happened immediately and I wasn't involved in trying to get this information in order to use it. I think this is a good example of the difference between concentrating and letting the understanding heal you.

Dr. Hora: Now, when we don't know the difference, we are seeking information. If we are seeking information, we will concentrate and accumulate information and frustrate ourselves. If we seek not information but inspiration, we will pay attention and we will understand. If something is disturbing to us, then it will disappear. We will suddenly find PAGL.

Student: What happens at that moment when all of the invalid concerns go? Is that something you can talk about or are we just to be grateful that it happens? Maybe it is not important. Maybe it is only important to know that when you are praying correctly there is a possibility that you can be healed. Can we go further and say what happens?

Dr. Hora: Well, we know that the source of all inspiration and creative ideas and healing solutions to our problems are inspired ideas reaching us from Divine Mind. If we are concentrating, we are not hearing God. We are just trying to figure things out for ourselves. We have no use for God because we are doing a "do-it-yourself" project. The whole world is concentrating most of the time, focusing on details, remembering, and relying on memory. Paying attention is sort of a meditative mode-of-being-in-the-world. We are just listening to ideas obtaining in consciousness. It is effortless, efficient and effective; but we have to "pay the duty" on it. We have to give up this urge to be smart. People who want to be smart cannot pay attention.

Student: What happens with individuals who seem to be stupid? For example, this year I'm teaching a wonderful class. Everybody can read and they enjoy reading. What they read they can communicate. You can teach them. Last year I had a class and they still couldn't read and they were ten and eleven years old. Their teacher just said to me the other day, "What is happening with them? They cannot read. They cannot do math." This is in spite of the tremendous effort that has been poured into the class. They go to corrective reading. They go to all these special programs.

Dr. Hora: Do they have computers in the class?

Student: No. They just don't seem to learn. So, what is happening?

Dr. Hora: Recently I was trying to study to use a computer and found myself very stupid because it required concentration. It is a different kind of attention, and I am not used to concentrating and accumulating information. It was very difficult for me and I still don't know how to do it. It is a different world. The handicap I am experiencing is the need for concentrating and accumulating information.

Student: It is interesting that you say that because I find that in a work environment we are required to be informed. So, there is an awful amount of effort in concentrating on the reading materials we have to read. I find I resent that. I prefer a more creative approach. I find there is a large element of that required in almost any kind of business environment. When you were just speaking, it occurred to me I resent this most of the time.

Dr. Hora: People complain about those manuals.

Student: (*Sighing*) They're awful!

Dr. Hora: Right? You must accumulate knowledge with manuals. You need to concentrate. It is like mental calisthenics. You have to know how to do this, but if you are learning how to use one of these machines, you need to become a technician. It is all right to become a technician when the need is for that; but essentially, we are spiritual divine consciousness. All our wisdom, our understanding, and healing come not through thinking but through listening—not through reading but through hearing. We hear the wisdom of God reaching us and every moment is precious and healing. We have to get healed from focusing attention on concentration.

There are some thinkers in the world today who say there are two kinds of people, and one kind is technically oriented people who concentrate on building useful machines. It is a very necessary skill to be able to concentrate and use predigested knowledge to function, but it is important to know that this is not our real life. We are not machines. Machines are useful but we become machine-like if we have not learned to pay attention and to develop our spiritual faculties of wisdom and love.

I saw two computer experts on television who are teachers. They have their schools. One of them said that he had made an interesting observation: those students who love their machines and develop a certain kind of love relationship with the computer learn very fast, but they almost humanize or attribute certain spiritual qualities to their particular computers. They approach it with an entirely different attitude than those students who have difficulty learning how to use the machines because to them the machine has no soul. You can apparently imagine that this machine has a soul, or at least you can develop some affection for the machine. Of course, this could be dangerous because you can start liking maybe your vacuum cleaner. (*Laughing*) You become an excellent housekeeper. (*Laughter*) So that is the answer to your problem. You have to love paying attention. That is where the intelligence comes from.

Now in the schools I don't think that the children are being taught to pay attention. They are taught to concentrate and accumulate. If you listen to the tapes of our groups, you also must not focus on the words of what is being said. Just allow the meaning to seep in. That is what you did and certainly it is very helpful.

Student: So then paying attention makes us receptive to the truth.

Dr. Hora: Absolutely. Yes. That is what happens in meditation. Somebody asked, "What should I meditate on?" I said, "How far you can spit with one spit ball." (*Laughter*) You see, meditation is completely abolishing this tendency to focus in on an issue. When you are focusing in on an issue, you are concentrating. It has its usefulness but that is not the creative aspect of our lives and it has its limitations and difficulties.

Student: Is that the meaning when I sit down to meditate and sometimes it is more helpful than others?

Dr. Hora: Yes.

Student: Sometimes we have to be alert to this effort of "concentrating" versus "allowing."

Dr. Hora: It has to be effortless, efficient and effective, right? In meditation we are not trying to concentrate on anything. Some people recommend concentrating on your breathing. It can get boring if you don't know what it means to meditate. In meditation we need

to be open with reverent receptivity to whatever comes into consciousness. Many people fall asleep. But with true meditation there
is no daydreaming; there is no concentration. Being receptive is a
special skill which we have to learn if we are involved in spiritual
studies. God doesn't have to think about anything. God already
knows everything.

Student: Sometimes I listen to a tape of one of these group dialogues
and I hear something that I have heard many times before, but I
am aware that this time I actually hear it in a way that I never did
before. Is that because I have suddenly become receptive, or is it
because I am not concentrating?

Dr. Hora: It is the same thing. If you are receptive, you are not concentrating.

Student: Sometimes I become receptive when I am suffering. I'm
forced by the suffering to be receptive. Is it that?

Dr. Hora: Usually suffering is a distraction. In order to meditate effec-
tively for a healing, we have to be able to transcend the suffering.
We have to disregard the pain or the aggravation sometimes. These
thoughts intrude themselves in consciousness and they are usually
about relationships. The greatest obstacle to meditation is relationships. If you have "relationships" you cannot meditate because you
are thinking about people. In meditation there are no people. There
are no persons. There is only God and we don't have a relationship
with God. If you think you have a "relationship" with God you are
not meditating; you are probably listening to some popular religious preacher.

Student: Would this also apply to reading inspired writings?

Dr. Hora: Yes, that kind of reading is very beneficial, very useful. Sure.

Life is a very complicated process, and if we don't understand
these fine details, then we just don't know what we are doing.
You see educated people, like our student here who is a Harvard
graduate, use concentration and attention interchangeably, without

realizing the difference. (*Addressing the student:*) I suppose it must have been a great surprise to you to hear that concentration is not the same as attention, right? In the schools they don't teach people to understand what they are doing. There are millions of people who "pray" and millions of people who "meditate" and millions of people who concentrate—and these millions of people just don't know what is happening.

Student: I am a little confused with the idea of paying attention. Are we saying that if we have a job that we need to do with a computer, for example, and we are grateful for this tool knowing we can get the work done faster using it—doesn't awareness play a part in that if we are aware of gratitude?

Dr. Hora: Yes, even that teacher of computers emphasized that the student has to develop a love for the machine.

Student: So, that is like gratitude then?

Dr. Hora: You could say that, surely. You have a positive attitude toward a very amazing machine, like the computer, and you are grateful for being able to use it and what you can produce with it; so you make peace.

Student: It doesn't have to be a struggle.

Dr. Hora: Yes. The famous philosopher Heidegger wrote a lot of articles and books about the problem of man's relationship to his machines. He recognized that more and more life is involved with very smart machines and man has to use them and still not become a machine himself. That is a great danger. If you don't understand this dichotomy between concentration and attention, you may become a machine yourself. You lose your soul. What profiteth a man who gains the world and loses his soul?[14] So he developed a slogan to protect his students: *Gelassenheit zu dein denken.* It

---

14 - "For what is a man profited, if he shall gain the whole world, and lose his own soul?" (Matthew 16:26)

Dr. Hora: Yes. We have to use these very useful, amazing machines, but we must not get attached to them—not turn them into idols and start worshiping the machine. If we start worshiping the machine, we become machines ourselves. Have you ever known such people that are very machine-like? They become rigid and like machines, and the ability for creative insight disappears.

Student: Is that the main problem then, that creativity is stifled?

Dr. Hora: Right. Of course, they lose the soul. There is no soul. There is only information, concentration and productivity. I think Charlie Chaplin made a movie about this.[15] The people who worked on these machines became machines themselves and lost their souls. So, it is very important to cherish our souls.

Student: Is it valid to think about paying attention? We always think about paying attention in terms of ceaseless prayer.

Dr. Hora: You have the blessing of studying Metapsychiatry which is cultivating "soul consciousness." There is "sense existence" and there is "soul existence". If we are getting swallowed up by technology, we develop sense existence. It is an entirely different life. If we are studying Metapsychiatry, we are learning to know ourselves as soul existence.

We have a student here who is a wonderful example of a balance between these two modes of being in the world. She is excellent with the machine but she is not absorbed; she has not become mechanical in her mode of being in the world. She has cultivated soul existence. You see, it is possible to function on both levels provided you know something about the human condition and the dangers

15 - *Modern Times* (1936)

that we must guard against. The Bible is always guarding against idolatry. When we develop idolatries, the Buddhists call it "attachment." Above all, don't get attached to anything because you are a spiritual being and you are here for God. Your attention has to be focused on being a transparency for God, and then you can do your wonderful computer work and everything else. You can cook...

Student: ...and clean house...

Dr. Hora: ...and clean the house. (*Laughter*) You can do this, but a balance has to be made with a clear emphasis on soul existence because in soul existence, there is creativity and there is healing and there is true love. But in sense existence, there is just technology. Seemingly there is a dividing line between technological existence and spiritual consciousness and if we don't know this, then there is confusion. If you listen to people talk, you can hear where they are living. Do they live in the computers or do they live in God, spiritual consciousness? There are some people who have completely abandoned the technological mode of being in the world and have become full-time meditators of soul existence.

I saw a movie on television about a group of people who were teaching "raja yoga." These men and women wear white flowing clothes, and spend many hours on a mountain side, sitting in certain cross-legged postures, looking straight ahead and meditating for hours on end. It seems like they are not interested in anything else but meditation. They are fully involved in the cultivation of their soul existence and they talk about "soul consciousness." The interesting thing that occurred to me as I was watching this and thinking about it, is that yoga includes physical exercises and one would have the idea that these are just the performance of physical feats of great interest. But, no, the practitioners have just learned to be comfortable in spite of the body so that they could lose awareness of the body. Many people think that the secret of enlightenment can be found by learning to sit cross-legged on the floor like the Buddha. That is nonsense. Cross-legged sitting developed in India because they had no chairs. (*Laughter*)

Anyway, don't worry about sitting cross-legged. Many people worry that they cannot twist themselves into this pretzel, but the fact is that these early, early Indians, even those who were not spiritually minded, found out that the only way to be able to sit comfortably without a chair or something to lean on is what they call the "lotus position." You can really sit comfortably for hours on end if you know how to sit in the lotus position. In raja yoga, at least the group which I saw on television, they are seeking soul consciousness. The emphasis is that man is a spiritual being and the most important aspect of that existence is the soul, and we have to cultivate the soul because we are in constant danger of being swallowed up by technology. But, it is still good to know how to drive a car. (*Laughter*) So, you see being a human is very complicated.

Student: In driving a car, though, it seems that you first concentrate to learn how to drive a car but then it becomes automatic.

Dr. Hora: The moment you see yourself as a "good driver" you have already been swallowed up by the car.

Student: So, the danger is if we are concentrating on driving, we are still turning attention to...

Dr. Hora: ...to the latest gossip on the radio. But of course, if you are an evolved spiritual consciousness, you are not interested in the gossip. You never turn on the radio either.

Student: Actually, there could be a lot of inspiration in all this machinery too—in the original idea, the way it is designed.

Dr. Hora: Right. Well, the creativity, the invention—certainly creativity has a lot to do with it; but again you are having a relationship with something that doesn't have a soul. We must not lose our soul. Jesus warned against that.

I read about a young man, his name is Bill Gates, and he has become a billionaire through creative thinking about software. He produced fantastic software. He is brilliant, 32 years old, and amazingly creative. He is involved with this technology. He is a miracle, this fellow. There are others in this field. Apparently, he is able to keep himself from becoming a victim of his own thought processes and computer technology.

Dr. Hora: (*Turning to one of the students*) Could you tell us how he does it?

Student: Well, I don't know whether he spends most of his time on the technical side or the marketing side. Marketing is the principal reason for the growth of the company. He is brilliant at marketing. Other companies have similar products and he is very clever at forming alliances with other companies.

Dr. Hora: He seems to have salvaged his soul, nevertheless. Because I have read about his participation and discussions with economists.

Student: I think most of the leaders in the computer field are very creative and certainly they use it as a tool. I don't see the danger that is described. Organizationally the danger exists. We might try to communicate with someone at a company and the response is , "The information is in the computer and it's lost." Bureaucratically there are problems but in actually using a computer, all the people around me appreciate the creativity. They themselves are creative. I don't see it as being a problem.

Dr. Hora: It's like driving a car. You could be a good driver of the car. Just don't become the car.

Student: I read a biography about Einstein, and as brilliant as he was he was considered very humble. He said things in simple statements. Sometimes I think the ability to concentrate is kind of like a feat of the mind. I tend to think, "I mastered that." However, in paying attention, I have to admit, "I don't know," and wait for an answer. The answer that comes is wonderful but I can't take any credit for it. I have to be humble. It is hard to be humble.

Dr. Hora: Yes.

Student: Is the same thing true with memory? If we have difficulty remembering things, is that the same as concentrating?

Dr. Hora: Sometimes people ask me, "Should I memorize the Bible? You can recite long passages from the Bible." They have accused me of this. (*Laughter*) The fact is that I have never read the Bible cover to cover—just snatches of certain passages I that I have seen in the Bible and they stayed with me. I have never tried to remember anything, not only from the Bible but also who owes me how much money. (*Laughter*) It is not necessary if you are oriented to this mode-of-being-in-the-world. You don't need to rely on memory. You rely on inspiration and whatever is needed to know or to write. God places it in your awareness. It is effortless, efficient and effective. Never, never try to memorize anything. That is why I was a lousy student in high school. They want memorizing in school. No, it is not necessary. What is worth remembering, will come up in the right moment. Sometimes it doesn't come up, which means you don't need it.

Student: Or you may not have been interested.

Dr. Hora: Right. God always provides what is needed—all the ideas, all the circumstances, all the opportunities. Everything is provided. If you need a parking space, it is provided, right? You didn't know that?

Student: So, the inspiration is acknowledging that there is Divine Mind?

Dr. Hora: Yes, that is very important because everything—if you look at the world, at business, at the technology which we are surrounded by—it always tells you, "You have to have a good mind." "You have to know things." "You have to be able to remember important information." That is how life looks on the surface, and it is very easy to become reliant on using our heads. If we use our head, we become stupid, but if we learn soul existence, we don't have to worry, "Will I remember? Won't I remember? Will I be able to do this or that?"

God is expressing himself through consciousness and all that is needed is always there. What we learn in Metapsychiatry is to know the difference of the two modes of being in the world. We cultivate the awareness of the *soul* which is a synonym for "God in manifestation." God is expressing himself through his creation and we are learning to appreciate this and be aware of it and function on a spiritual level rather than on a material level.

Student: The soul is a manifestation of God. Is that what you said?

Dr. Hora: Soul is one of the many disguises of God. You are another one. God is disguising himself in the universe as individual life. We don't say, "God and man" or "Man in God." We say, "God *in* man. God *as* man." We don't say, "Man as God." We say, "God as man." People who make this mistake are being accused of megalomania. What is "megalomania?"

Student: Delusions of grandeur.

Dr. Hora: Delusions of grandeur. We don't say, "I am God;" we say, "God is me." God is in me. God is through me. God is me, but I am *not* God. Is it clear? Jesus said, "I and my Father are one. I am in the Father and the Father in me."[16] We say, "I am a transparency for God. God is expressing himself through me as Love-Intelligence all the time." The soul, which can be recognized everywhere where there is life—this soul is God in manifestation. God as man.

Many religions make the mistake of saying man is an animal and a sinner. The only man who was different than we are was Jesus Christ and he was God. He was an exceptional character. Jesus was God.

---

16 - John 10:30 and John 14:11)

7

Concept of God

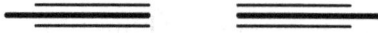

───── ─────

Student: I reread the book of Ecclesiastes in the Bible this week. It seems to say there is no sense in trying to accomplish anything; you just live out your life. That seems to be the message.

Dr. Hora: And then you die, they bury you in a grave, and it is all forgotten, and it was for naught, right? This is called the philosophy of nihilism. That is not what the book is saying.

Student: I think the part that says there is no point in trying to accomplish anything is saying—

Dr. Hora: No. We have to accomplish everything possible, but we accomplish it for the good of God. Ecclesiastes speaks of himself, and he believed that you had to enjoy life to the fullest and build things so you could brag about it, because he was vain. If we misunderstand life in terms of personal vanity, then our lives are futile—good for nothing—or, as Jesus put it, "to be cast out and trodden underfoot" (Matthew 5:13). Ecclesiastes is a very helpful book. Life can be futile, absolutely. If we live life without any reference to a higher power and a higher wisdom and a higher purpose, it is a misconception.

Student: Is there any mention of God in Ecclesiastes?

Dr. Hora: Did you find any?

Student: There was. I don't exactly remember the context. The book seemed to be driving toward an answer.

Dr. Hora: Yes, it is evident that he was a hedonist. He was very rich. He had many wives, concubines, palaces all over the place. He had servants and gardeners. He had everything that, from a materialistic perspective, life has to offer. He didn't have a television set, but he had his pornography right there at the flick of a finger to bring in the ladies of the night. It is a very instructive book, and it shows the futility and the frustration of an individual who is just self-seeking and whose aim in life is self-gratification. He didn't find that there is a higher purpose to our being here. It's sad. Even now there are millionaires who are miserable all the time.

Student: I understood him to say something like, "Cursed is the man who is given everything but is not given the ability to appreciate joy."

Dr. Hora: But everybody has the ability. What he needed was somebody to set him straight—maybe an article on Metapsychiatry. (*Laughter*)

I just met with a young Japanese lady and I asked her, "Are you Buddhist?" She said no. "Are you Christian?" She said no. "Are you Jewish?" She said no. "Are you Shinto?" She said no. I said, "What are you?" She said, "I don't know." She is a college graduate, and she had no conception of the possibility that there must be a God someplace. She grew up in Japan totally unaware and uneducated about God, which is absolute agnosticism. I don't know if you can find an absolute agnostic. There are atheists, there are Communists, but this girl had a total absence of knowledge of God, of the existence of a Divine Reality. I was amazed. How is it possible you can grow up not knowing that there is the *possibility* of God? There are people who ignore God, but in our world it is impossible to be a total agnostic, an innocent. She didn't reject it. She just had no idea there could be a God. It is a very rare phenomenon. Usually people are mad at God or disgusted with God or afraid of God, or they hate God or fight against God. This poor girl suffers tremendous anxieties. It is immobilizing her. It is really not possible to live without God, because even if you deny God or if you reject God, you are involved with God. It is not possible to live without God.

Student: There are misconceptions about God.

Dr. Hora: Those are religious misconceptions. You are still involved with God. You can be involved negatively, or positively, or ignorantly or fearfully or superstitiously or religiously, but you are still involved with God.

If you don't have a concept of God, you cannot really live, because whether you are religious or not, you are constantly praying to your own god. Everybody has his own god. With some people it is money or power, automobiles or whatever. Whatever you cherish or whatever you hate or whatever you fear, that is your god, and you are constantly praying to it.

Student: In the case of someone who doesn't have a concept of God, which individual would be more receptive to learning: someone with a misconception, or someone with no concept at all?

Dr. Hora: That is really not the problem. What makes it possible to teach someone is discomfort, and she has great discomfort, because she is fearful of everything and has no sense of direction. You have to have some pain to become interested in God. There is no shortage of pain. The Bible says, "They are without excuse" (Romans 1:20). She had never seen a Bible. She grew up in Japan, on an island where there are no Christians. There are probably Shintoists and Buddhists. She has never seen a Bible, and she doesn't know anything about the existence of God. She is a genuine innocent. I asked, "How about your parents? Aren't they religious?" She said, "Once a year a priest will come to the house and perform a ceremony so nobody will die." In the family, it is a habit to call a priest to sprinkle some holy water and burn some incense. But she never knew anything about why they do this. This is a totally innocent young lady.

Student: Isn't that rather common? I find it frequently among the faculty in the school where I teach.

Dr. Hora: They are all rejecting the concept of God. They are not innocent. This young lady is a genuine innocent, which I have never met before in my life. You can be for it or against it or love it or hate it, but to be completely oblivious of the existence of God…it is hard to imagine that somebody can survive that way.

Student: She has no myths?

Dr. Hora: Absolutely nothing. She has tremendous discomfort—fear, fear of life.

There is a very famous lady who claims she is an atheist. I don't know if she is still preaching her religion. Atheism can be a religion. If you proclaim yourself an atheist, this means you are religious because you are worshiping an idea that there is no God; therefore, there is God. If there were no God, you couldn't reject God. This young lady doesn't reject God. She just doesn't know of the possibility that God exists.

Student: You said that everyone is constantly praying. Do you have a clue as to what this young lady is praying for?

Dr. Hora: No. It was just a short interview. I haven't found out anything. She must be praying to something. I have aroused in her a curiosity about how life can be lived *with* God or *without* God. She came to see me to find out why she is so afraid. She lives in fear, with anxieties constantly tormenting her. She cannot communicate with people. She doesn't know whether she is coming or going. It is suffering—the discomfort in all of us—that leads us to consider the possibility of the existence of God. We go further and usually we find the wrong god to live by (*Laughing*), but at least it's something—better than nothing. A wrong god is better than no god at all. Now, Ecclesiastes believed that feeling good is a sign of being a godly man, so he developed his own religion of hedonism. That was his god. We could all ask ourselves, "What is my god?" We usually find the wrong god. It takes laborious study and help to find the right God.

Student: Something we've discussed many times before is that everyone has to find God and everyone seems to think they have to do something—like a ritual or something.

Dr. Hora: A ritual will not help you to find God.

Student: I know, but I saw a movie recently that showed many world religions, and what struck me was that there appeared to be a tremendous urge to *do* something, to ritualize. Is this a way of trying to get a handle on God?

Dr. Hora: Exactly right. Jesus explained that most people don't understand God. They would like to, but the human tendency is to become superstitious and develop fantasies. Or, if you are a "proactive person" you can figure out an activity, and say, "Well, God likes it if I tap my nose" or something. Some people develop complicated ceremonies and rituals, and they get caught up in them. Joggers will start jogging and cannot stop. Have you heard about that? There are many joggers to whom jogging has become a religion, and they are afraid to stop. There are all kinds of activities used in this way.

Now, the knowledge of God is not an activity. No kind of activity is going to help you to know God. Even in Buddhism many believe that sitting *zazen*, meditating while sitting cross-legged, will help you to find God. No way will it help you to find God. God can only be found in consciousness, and when God is found in consciousness, you are not *doing* anything. You are just opening up the "third eye," which means you begin to appreciate awareness. As awareness is expanding, you discover an entirely different Reality. In this Reality, all things work together for good. Then you have found it. It is spiritual bliss—bliss consciousness. God can only be found in consciousness. It's not in a book, it's not in a relationship, it's not in mountain climbing, and it's not found in a ritual or some activity or ceremony. It is a quality of awareness. And that makes all the difference.

Student: How is this awareness attained?

Dr. Hora: With the First Principle of Metapsychiatry.[1] It is very simple. You constantly monitor your thought and ask yourself, "What am I primarily interested in at this moment?" If it is some other nonsense, you know you are not on the beam, and you quickly retire, return to the beam, by contemplating the First Principle with utmost sincerity. That is how we develop an awareness of the presence and nature of God, Divine Reality.

Student: I was reading about gratitude and how it is important to be grateful and have gratitude not only when things are positive, but especially when they are negative. When things are going bad, it seems too hard to be grateful.

Dr. Hora: Be grateful for the negative, and if it leads you to the positive, then it is easy.

Student: It seems that when things are going bad, I'm going *away* from God rather than being grateful. How do I turn that around?

Dr. Hora: It is a gradual process of first learning to be aware of what you are thinking, and then learning to be aware of the meaning of what is happening to you. For instance, recently I went into a store to buy something (it was an Arabic store, but I didn't know that at the time), and I was trying to talk to the salesman in English. While he was serving me, behind me was another man, and he was talking in Arabic to the salesman who was trying to serve me, and the salesman didn't hear what I was saying. I couldn't talk with him. The whole situation was very unpleasant, because they completely drowned me out in their private conversation, which I couldn't understand. The transaction was getting messed up. They were carrying on a conversation in Arabic in total disregard of my presence. I had an experience of being completely annihilated. So

1 - The First Principle of Metapsychiatry: "Thou shalt have no other interests before the good of God, which is spiritual blessedness."

I asked myself, "What is the meaning of this?" Immediately my reaction was to think, "These Arabs don't like me." (*Laughter*) But then I caught myself. (*Laughing*) "Well, if this is happening to me, it must have another meaning." I had to become aware of my thoughts about these men. I rejected my negative attitude, and turned to the good of God, which is universally present and is harmonious. Everything righted itself right then and there. There was no more problem. The salesman was suddenly interested in understanding me. The discomfort was healed. I didn't waste time finding fault with the Arabs. I found the fault in my thoughts.

Student: You could see the meaning for you and then turn.

Dr. Hora: How else can you heal yourself? How else can you contribute to healing the Arab-Israeli conflict? (*Laughter*) You have to know the meaning. Absolutely.

Student: You have to be willing to let the meaning reveal itself.

Dr. Hora: Of course. It is so much easier to blame someone else.

Student: The more we develop this habit of examining our thoughts in the context of a situation, the easier it becomes to see the meaning.

Dr. Hora: We have the great blessing of the Eleven Principles, which help us to turn away from the meaning to a valid thought. We become aware of this, and things are healed.

Student: Without awareness, we constantly run into these situations and blame others, and tomorrow the same thing happens all over again.

Dr. Hora: That explains the sorry condition of the world. Everyone is finding fault with everyone else, and there is no resolution of the situation. "First cast the beam out of thine own eye and then shalt thou see to remove the mote from your brother's eye" (Matthew 7:5). It is all in the Bible, you know. It is very helpful to know the Bible—in the right way of course, not in the literal way.

Student: What does that mean? How can you "cast out the mote from your brother's eye" if your brother is not interested?

Dr. Hora: You cannot, but if you have successfully removed the beam from your own eye, your brother might ask you to help him. That can happen.

Student: So is awareness defined as "consciousness of the content of consciousness"?

Dr. Hora: Yes. Surely.

Student: I was just thinking about the example you gave of being in the shop. I would probably be tempted to try to figure it out and think of some statement to address the problem. Such an intellectual exercise is futile. Is this what you call mental vanity?

Dr. Hora: Yes, it is intellectual vanity. Intellectual vanity assumes that everyone else is wrong and you have the mind power to fix it.

Student: It is humbling to sit and wait for the answer. It is easier to try to figure it out than wait for the answer to come to you.

Dr. Hora: Yes, that is what everybody else is doing. They figure it out— "What is wrong with those guys?"—but nothing changes, and there is no peace.

Student: If you had just walked away without purchasing anything, that would have been avoiding the issue, not addressing it.

Dr. Hora: Right. I could sulk for a while. (*Laughter*) That is no solution.

Student: Is that what transcendence is—the situation that you described? You are in a situation where things are not going so well, and then there is some awareness of the Truth.

Dr. Hora: Yes, you could call it transcendence. You replace human evaluation of the situation with a spiritual evaluation. Whenever spirit transcends the human condition, we have transcendence. It is not psychology; it is transcendence.

Student: Is the faculty that is aware of an invalid idea the same faculty as the one that sees the Truth of Being?

Dr. Hora: Yes. There is a passage in the Bible that says, " There is neither Jew nor Greek, there is neither bond nor free, there is neither male nor female: for ye are all one in Christ Jesus" (Galatians 3:28-29). It is the transcendent view of the human condition. People are judging from all kinds of vantage points, but they are always judging rather than rising above the human scene and allowing themselves to be aware of the Christly perspective on Reality. That is transcendence. We look at life through the eyes of Jesus Christ or the Buddhist monk Huineng What did Huineng say? He said, "From the beginning, nothing is." Isn't that a Christly statement? (*Laughter*) What was he saying?

Student: "Nothing is as it seems to be; neither is it otherwise."[2]

Dr. Hora: Right. Exactly.

Student: Please explain, "neither is it otherwise."

Dr. Hora: To explain the end would be to rob you of an opportunity to agonize and become enlightened. It would be sinful. To explain a koan is a sin. What makes it a sin?

Student: It's like cheating.

Dr. Hora: Right. The koan has a purpose which is to enlighten people spontaneously. We have spoken earlier about spontaneity[3]. The understanding of the koan requires spontaneity, which means it has to be God who tells you the message in the koan. No human reasoning or intellectualism will ever assist you in becoming enlightened.

There have been people who thought they could do this. They collected many koans that Zen masters had used in their teaching over the years. They offered these with explanations and interpretations in a published a book. That book is a sin, because people who read

---

2 - A Zen koan attributed to Alan Watts

3 - For example, see: Session 8, "Spontaneity", *Encounters with Wisdom, Book One.*

those koans are like spoiled children and will never become enlightened. Rather than wait for God to reach their consciousness so
that they see the light they want it handed to them. It is like when
a caterpillar is struggling to come out of the pupa stage to become
a butterfly. If someone assists this caterpillar in taking it out of its
pupa, it collapses and dies. Sometimes being helpful is not helpful.
The struggle is necessary. So, nothing is as it seems to be, but neither is it otherwise—very frustrating! (*Laughing*)

Student: You have said that growth and understanding come either from
suffering or through wisdom, and yet it seems that in most cases
they come through suffering. The idea that they come through wisdom is puzzling. Is it possible to reach a point where we no longer
need problems and suffering?

Dr. Hora: We mustn't be afraid of suffering. You know, it is a tremendous relief to learn that *all* suffering has a meaning. How terrible
it would be if there were no explanation—just pain and suffering,
and it is hopeless, and it is going to get worse and worse. But, if
you have studied Metapsychiatry, you know it doesn't have to get
worse; it is *never* hopeless, and *everything* has a meaning. If you
are sufficiently sincere in looking for the meaning, it will reveal
itself to you, and there will be healing. You don't have to be a helpless victim of suffering. God has not ordained suffering. Suffering
occurs just if you don't know.

The Japanese girl is suffering a great deal. She has no idea that this
doesn't have to be. If you have no idea that it doesn't have to be,
then you are in a hopeless situation, and you continue from bad to
worse. There is a great relief for all students of Metapsychiatry if
we remember that we don't have to be oppressed victims of suffering. It only takes a little intestinal fortitude. (That's an interesting
phrase somebody has invented (*Laughing*) —"intestinal fortitude.")
We need to face up to the meaning of the problem and turn around.
As Jesus said, "Turn around, the Kingdom of God is at hand."[4]

---

4 - "From that time Jesus began to preach, and to say, 'Repent: for the kingdom of heaven is

Student: This is a tremendous freedom, and only someone who studies Metapsychiatry would ever know that.

Dr. Hora: It has been a well-kept secret from the beginning of time. People have been suffering and thinking it is inevitable, incurable, and terminal —in an interminable way!

What makes it so difficult for man to be sincere? It is really amazing. Some people find it impossible to be sincere.

Student: We are miseducated and we think we should be a certain way, and if we are not that way, people won't accept us.

Dr. Hora: Right, and sometimes we don't understand ourselves. We are caught up in a resistance to sincerity, which could save our lives.

Student: I wouldn't trust myself to say, "I am sincere," because I wouldn't believe it!

Dr. Hora: You couldn't be sincere in a sincere way. That is what Ecclesiastes meant when he said, "Vanity of vanities. All is vanity and vexation of spirit." [5] Vanity is too vain to admit that it is vain. That is a real screw-up.

Now, there is a famous story in the Bible. (2 Kings, Chapter 5) A Syrian military man named Naaman came down with leprosy, and he was advised to go see a Jewish teacher of Metapsychiatry. His name was Elisha. As Naaman approached, Elisha sent out a messenger and told him, "Stop there. Don't come closer." Naaman sent his servant to Elisha to explain that he had leprosy and he had come to be healed because he had heard that Elisha could heal people. Elisha said, "If you want to be healed, you have to dunk yourself seven times into the River Jordan." Naaman's answer was, "What, *me*, a Syrian, dunk myself into this Jewish river seven times? No way am I going to do that!" He was very proud. You see, the prophet wanted him to reveal himself and become aware of this

---

at hand.' " (Matthew 4:17)

5 - These phrases appear throughout the book of Ecclesiastes.

inordinate pride. Naaman struggled. He turned to leave, but those around him begged him: "Look here, if you don't give into this request, you will die." It was a very serious disease. Finally, after much hesitation (he went through hell deciding to obey this order) he did it. He dunked himself seven times in the river and came out completely healed. He was very grateful afterward and tried to send gifts of money and things to the prophet. Elisha rejected his gifts and said, "I wouldn't defile myself with your stuff. (*Laughter*) I am too proud." (*Laughter*) —That's *my* version. (*Laughing*)

8

Beyond The Physical

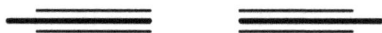

Student: How can we come to understand that we are what we really are—spiritual beings and not physical bodies? Is there a way that we can facilitate this understanding, or is it something that just has to awaken in us like other things we have talked about?

Dr. Hora: Well, if you have read *Beyond the Dream,* you may have come across a chapter titled "The Physical Is Mental." Now, how can that be?

Student: I have seen that proven over and over again. I mean, it is not for lack of examples or demonstrations. I see the relationship all the time between thoughts and physical symptoms. I was thinking about the pain that I have in one of my ribs. I don't know if it is broken or what. It seems that when I move in a certain way, it hurts. So, overcoming cause-and-effect thinking, knowing that the pain is a thought doesn't seem to be enough. I need real understanding that we are spiritual, which would give me the ability to turn away from the physical. That's very difficult.

Dr. Hora: Now, what do you think? Anybody?

Student: I was just wondering if part of it is working on seeing how we confirm ourselves as physical, and that we have a choice. We don't *have* to confirm ourselves as physical. There is such a thing as God-consciousness—but we keep worrying about how much we sleep and how we eat—all these physical things. It's the whole way we think. That seems to be a part of it.

Dr. Hora: So, we can have the information, on good authority, that the physical is mental, and we can believe it is so, because we believe the source of that information. Then we have all kinds of demonstrations— experiences, let's say, where we see that when the mental is healed and a certain thought is healed, the physical symptom disappears. But what would happen if we would completely understand this claim that the physical is mental?

Student: That would be a great liberation, and in addition the symptoms would disappear, because symptoms thrive on attention.

Dr. Hora: Yes. Do you know what would happen if we would really understand this—completely? We would disappear. You don't want that to happen (*Laughing*). But we can understand it to the degree that physical problems can disappear, and we have many examples here; everybody's had healings. To the extent that we understand something, we get healed, we get freedom, we get the wisdom not to be bamboozled and intimidated by every little scratch and itch, and an accident or discordant situation is not devastating for us. Millions of people run to hospitals and emergency rooms all the time, worried and fearful—with all kinds of symptoms—and the more you run for the alleviation of symptoms, the more frightened you become and the more you are giving in to these fears and thoughts, and life is just one continuous agony.

The word "agony" is very interesting. What is the derivation of the word "agony"?

Student: Is it "without knowing"?

Dr. Hora: Right. If you are completely ignorant of the Truth of Being, your life is a continuous agony. You are scared of everything. I know a couple who very much rely on medical care. Now, about a month ago, the doctor said, "It would be a good idea for you to get vaccinated against the flu." So, they ran and got themselves vaccinated against the flu, and then, in a few weeks, both of them came down with the flu. They told the doctor, and he said, "Well, the vaccination was good and it has protected many, but there is another kind of flu against which you didn't get a vaccination." This is an example of unenlightened life. It is in constant fear with constant rationalizations and excuses, and running from one doctor to another, et cetera.

Jesus mentioned that he had great compassion for people because they were like sheep without a shepherd, living in fear, without any direction, chaotic and vulnerable.[17] That's how life is if you have not begun to understand that the physical is mental. There is absolutely no protection, no meaning. Life doesn't make any sense. You are reaching out for this drug, for that thing, for that fad. People buy machines to exercise with. The whole world is just running scared, trying this and trying that.

So, when life consists of a continuous search for the Truth, and every day is a new day for us to deepen our understanding of the Truth of Being, to the point that we catch glimpses of the Truth of Being, we are healed of some problems. They disappear. If we would completely understand the Truth of Being, we would completely disappear. Wouldn't that be fun? (*Laughter*)

Student: Is it that idea that makes us reluctant sometimes to let go of certain problems?

Dr. Hora: No. To the human mind, the idea that the physical is mental, that the physical is nonmaterial, is absurd. Who will believe it? (*Laughing*) And if you try to *believe* it, that's no help. You have to *know* that there is this Truth that has to be eventually reached, and to every little degree that we have reached it we are greatly blessed. Fear is relieved, and we are healed and things resolve themselves. Problems just disappear.

Student: I don't know if I understand things or I just have faith in what you say.

---

17 - See: Matthew 9:36 , Mark 6:34

Dr. Hora: You believe Hora. That is an elementary mistake (*Laughing*). But it's better than nothing, right?

Student: Yes, but I keep thinking that I understand something but I don't think I really do. I think I am just accepting what you say.

Dr. Hora: If you don't understand, you don't have a healing.

Student: Isn't there such a thing as "faith healing"?

Dr. Hora: Well, faith healing is hypnotism, and it is worse than nothing, because you become addicted to something that is not valid.

Student: So, if any of us experience healing while working with you, there has to be some understanding of the Truth in order to be healed.

Dr. Hora: The understanding is never complete. If it were complete, we would ascend. That is the meaning of ascension. It took Jesus about three years to understand, and when that came to happen, he disappeared.

Student: If we say that the physical is mental, what is a healthy physical body? Is there any tangible "healthy stuff?" Is it all a thought about "health?"

Dr. Hora: There is neither sickness nor health.

Student: Is that in the spiritual realm? So, there is no physical anything, and God doesn't know about our health, either?

Dr. Hora: Of course not. God doesn't know "healthy people" and "sick people." There is only perfection. Do you remember what the Zen master said to his student when he hit the target? [18] He said, "Let us bow to perfection." He didn't say, "Thank God that this arrow found its target." He said, "Let us bow to perfection." Isn't that beautiful? The moment you say, "Thank God," you have an idol. You are idolizing a concept of God. But we can say, "God doesn't think in terms of "health and sickness," or "yes and no," and "good

---

18 - See: *Zen in the Art of Archery* , by Eugen Herrigel, 1948.

and bad." God is perfection. Perfect God, perfect universe, and perfect spiritual creation.

Yesterday I saw a movie about penguins. There are beautiful, big penguins that live in Antarctica. It is a fantastic manifestation of life. Who could have thought of the process of their lives? They live in this tremendously cold area, and how do they procreate? They copulate once a year, and the female produces an egg and the male takes the egg from the female and sits on it for nine months, and in these nine months he loses 40 percent of his weight. He cannot move anywhere. He is just protecting this egg in the process of its germinating into another penguin. After nine months, when the egg has turned into a little chick, the female comes back and pushes the male away and sits on it, and from then on, the female nurtures this offspring, because she has become fat and big, eating for nine months while the male was starving. That's how this whole process of life goes on. Nobody taught them how to do it. It is just a higher intelligence that evolved into this kind of life form. It is fascinating. They all knew what to do…without having to learn. It's a joint participation in the reproductive process.

Student: The camera people stayed around there all that time?

Dr. Hora: Yes, they did. They photographed every step of the way. Amazing.

Student: Was Jesus' demonstration of walking on water and passing through crowds and doors kind of a stepping-stone to his demonstration of the insubstantiality of matter?

Dr. Hora: Well, it's hard for us to say, because we haven't seen it. It is just described, and there is just information, and the question is, is this information valid? Is it complete? Did it really happen, and if it did happen, what could be the meaning of it? And we must also keep in mind that maybe it didn't happen. Maybe it was just a fantasy of the scribes. So, we are grateful for these records, and these descriptions, and we try to understand what they could mean, and it can be very helpful if some understanding comes to us from them, but we don't just accept the scriptures verbatim. We have to validate it in our own life experience. So, we don't argue against it, but we reserve judgment until an occasion arises in which the meaning of these stories becomes clear to us by virtue of the fact that something happens in our lives. If we read that Jesus walked on water[19], it doesn't mean necessarily that he walked on water. It may mean that he had dominion over the elements. It wouldn't make sense for such a great man as Jesus to perform a circus act and say, "Look what I can do! Look, Ma, no hands!" (*Laughter*)

Metapsychiatry says, "Don't believe nobody or nothing (*Laughter*), and don't disbelieve." I knew someone who suffered for years from wanting to trust. She was mistrusting and was caught up in whether she should trust or not trust. She couldn't find her peace until she could see that the whole thing didn't make any sense. We don't trust anybody, and we don't mistrust anybody. We wait until an understanding happens to us. Then there is no problem. Now, there are people who take literally every sentence and every word in the Bible, but we have to be careful about it. We are grateful for that book and the messages, but whatever we are interested in sincerely will validate itself in some way in our lives, and when that happens, we don't have to believe anything. Everything becomes clear.

Jesus fed the multitudes, he performed miracles, he healed the sick. All these things are fine, yes? Very nice. We don't argue about it. We don't say "I don't believe," and we don't say "I believe." *I am waiting.* Heidegger was famous for having said, "I am waiting for God." Some people accused him, a Catholic priest, of being blasphemous or of being an atheist or an agnostic. No. When they asked him, "What is your stand on the issue of God?" He said: "As far as God is concerned, I am waiting for Him." And that's right, because it is an arrogant thing to say, "I believe this," and it's equally arrogant to say, "I don't believe it." And if you approach Bible studies with an attitude of *I have got to believe this,* you'll never get anywhere.

19 - See: Matthew 14:25

Student: You said earlier that if God is perfection, if we are grateful for an event that occurs, and say, "Thank you, God," then, if I understood what you said, that separates ourselves from the idea of God because it is a concept of "self and God."

Dr. Hora: Yes.

Student: So how can you see a blessing in your life where that doesn't occur?

Dr. Hora: We have to be careful with God, because if we speak easily about God, maybe we are just wishful thinkers or superstitious, using God as an excuse to justify our religion. "God" is a religious word. When the Zen master said, "Let us bow to perfection," that was closer to the truth than all the religions together. Of course, it's not a crime to say, "Thank you, God." It just comes naturally. But if you are a profound thinker, you ask yourself, *What did I just say, and what does it mean when I say that?* It would be nice to have a "big daddy" who is here for us. If you say, "Thank you, God," you are saying, "This time, God, you were here for me. (*Laughter*) I feel good about you." But in Metapsychiatry we say, "God is not here for us. We are here for God."

Student: So, when good occurs, then we have to acknowledge that it is an extension of the Truth of Being.

Dr. Hora: Yes, it can be to us a demonstration that there is such a thing as the principle of infinite good, love, and intelligence that is often called God.

Student: So that validates the Truth?

Dr. Hora: Yes. God is a badly misused concept, and it is easy to talk about God, and we do. We do because language is insufficient to convey the immensity of divine perfection and goodness.

Student: What would be a way of seeing God in everything, in the beauty, rather than saying, "Thank you?"

Dr. Hora: You can say, "Thank you." It is an acknowledgment that there must be a principle of infinite good—God's good. But we have to be careful not to personalize God. God is not a person. God is a cosmic principle. Right?

When the Muslims are praying, they say, "There is no god but God." What are they saying? They are saying God is not a concept. It is a reality beyond everything else—which is right. You find these glimpses of Truth everywhere, not only in Zen but here and in Islam.

Student: When the Buddha gave the "Flower Sermon," he said nothing; he just held up a flower. Only one of disciples understood what was being conveyed. What was it that was understood by that one individual?

Dr. Hora: Anybody can say, "God is," but not everybody can say, "Beauty is," right? You look at the flower and you see beauty. You can be directly aware of beauty, but if you are someone selling flowers, you might only see merchandise, not beauty.

Student: You said it is not so easy to understand the idea that "God is"?

Dr. Hora: Right. Because we cannot sink our teeth into it.

Student: So, God is revealing Itself in the beauty?

Dr. Hora: Yes. Beauty is a quality of God. Truth is a quality of God. All the spiritual values are qualities of God. And the Zen master bows to perfection. It's a nonpersonal, nondimensional reality. This can be understood, but the human mind, which is not sophisticated in spiritual understanding, likes to make everything a concept, or a tangible reality, or a person—personification.

Student: What do we do with the human mind? I mean, do we outgrow it? Do we realize it is not real? Can it be used? What is it?

Dr. Hora: Well, the human mind must be used until we understand that there is only one Mind, which is God—Divine Mind, infinite wisdom and intelligence.

Today there was an interesting scene on one of the talk shows. A panel of white supremacists were arguing about Blacks and Whites and racism, saying, "There are Black people and there are White people, and they shouldn't be mixed." They were very hostile and argumentative, and they were trying to resolve the problem of racism, and of course these bigoted people have only one solution: "Let all the nonwhites get killed and eliminated." They were convinced that this is right. In the audience was a Black man, and he got up and said, "There is only intelligence or ignorance. All people are people, and it is hopeless to talk about 'Blacks' and 'Whites' and 'Yellows'—about races. Everybody is a human being, but human beings can be intelligent or they can be ignorant. That is all there is."

The others didn't like it. They were furious. But he was right. That's the truth. Either you know or you don't know, but you cannot judge by appearances. "Judge not by appearances" (John 7:24). All these mixed-up people are judging by appearances. How long will it take for the world to understand that there are no racial differences? There's only intelligence and ignorance. If this would be realized, it would solve the whole problem.

Years ago there was a student of Metapsychiatry, a lovely young woman, who was Jewish but was very interested in Catholicism. One day she went to a church and stood in line for the communion wafer. She was interested to find out what it was. When she came to the priest, he noticed that she was Jewish, and he said, "You cannot have this, because you are Jewish. You cannot get this blessing. You are not entitled to it." And the poor girl got so embarrassed, she ran out of church. This is a stupid, stupid kind of religious bigotry. She was sincerely trying to find out what it was.

Student: When I come here, it seems what you say is the truth. It all seems so hopeful that there is a way out of all these dualities, the dilemma of life. Yet being out in the world, it seems hopeless sometimes. There is just so much ignorance. It's difficult.

Dr. Hora: But you are not responsible for the ignorance of your parents or your friends or the people in business. You are not responsible for that. You just recognize it. They judge by appearances, and they don't understand. There are two kinds of people: there are intelligent people and ignorant people.

Student: But it all feels hopeless.

Dr. Hora: It is not up to you to cure all these ignorant people—you will have too many patients. (*Laughter*) You couldn't handle that.

Student: I always had this idea that I could really make a difference. (*Laughter*)

Dr. Hora: You would like to be a do-gooder. Look what happened to Jesus when he tried to convert the world. They crucified him. It is dangerous. There are many ways to get crucified, even today.

Student: So, we are to just see the suffering and not think we have to be involved personally?

Dr. Hora: Well, we see it and let God handle it. It is not for you to do it. But if somebody asks you, "Are you Jewish?" this question is a sign of racism and religious intolerance. Such people want to find something they like or don't like about someone else and to judge them. This is always going on. People are always trying to find out if someone is Black or White or this or that—maybe a Yankees fan? (*Laughter*) People have these totally insane concerns. What the heck? So much suffering comes from it. People are scared. If they apply for a job, they are examined—background, foreground, sideways—and not whether there is intelligence and there is "know-how;" yet that is all that matters. But the world has different criteria, which are existentially invalid.

Student: In business, it is kind of a practice every time someone new comes into the department...

Dr. Hora: They want to find out everything.

Student: Yes, I work for the city. They post it on the city emails, they post it within our group; 400 people are reading about their biography and where they came from, who they are or what they are. (*Laughter*) So that kind of activity, what does it do? It stirs up comparison thinking.

Dr. Hora: Sure, sure—and intolerance. People want to know something with which they could possibly damage somebody in case there is competition. Then they can get rid of the competition. They have to find something. Even President Clinton is being subjected to these kinds of shenanigans. They want to know whether he profited from a real estate deal 10 years ago. There's always something.

Student: You said that when we see the ignorance of the world, we let God handle it; it's not our job. How do you let God handle it? If the world is ignorant, how can God handle it? I don't see how God enters into the picture.

Dr. Hora: You want to know how He operates?

Student: No. Not how He is going to handle it, but how *could* God handle it? How could this principle of good handle the ignorance that has no awareness of the good and no interest in it and no desire to even come to know it? How can that principle handle it?

Dr. Hora: How can the sun shine on so many people at the same time?

Student: Half the people are not even aware that it is sunny. They are not paying attention.

Student: In one of my first sessions with Dr. Hora, my question was about how I handled a certain situation. And it was made clear to me that there *is* no handling. (*Laughter*) It is allowed to be. There is no such thing as "manipulating" or "handling," and I would think it would be an error to think that God handles anything.

Dr. Hora: Yes. When we say, "Let God handle it," it is just a facetious remark, because it dares to bring to our attention the fact that we are not God. It comes as a surprise. (*Laughter*)

Student: Is that always the issue, though—when we want to do something, we want to be something, we are taking the position of being God? Is that always the case?

Dr. Hora: Sure. That's the "should thinker." If you understand the Second Principle[20], then you have no problem letting God do His job.

Student: Is Divine Mind like the sun, reaching consciousness whether we are ignorant or not? If Divine Mind is the only Mind and we are blessed enough to realize what is a divine idea, we are blessed by this idea. But it is reaching every consciousness. It is like the sun is shining. So, to the extent that someone is somehow receptive, then God...

Dr. Hora: "Somehow receptive." Most people are not receptive, right? We have the power to ignore God. That is an interesting thing. We have the power to ignore God, which is a weakness. We can become atheists, or communists or self-righteous willful people who imagine that we have power to do things. This is an ignorance. It is a great weakness, and invariably it results in some tragedy.

Student: In one of the sessions a few weeks ago, we talked about backsliding. Backsliding—isn't that ignoring God?

Dr. Hora: Right, sure. Yes.

Student: We forgot about what we learned.

Dr. Hora: And we never learned enough. (*Laughter*)

Student: What amazes me is that with all that learning, we could even consider *not* thinking about God. Is it always the sense that we are not thoroughly convinced that we have no power or that we can't make a difference or we can't do something?

Dr. Hora: Yes. You see, this is so slippery when you say "thinking about God." Thinking *about* God doesn't do much. There are many religious people who think about God all the time. They argue

---

20 - The Second Principle of Metapsychiatry: "Take no thought for what should be or what should not be; seek ye first to know the good of God, which already is."

about God and contend theologically, and it's always "God, God, God, God, God."

Student: They are not aware.

Dr. Hora: Not aware. Yes. We have to learn to be aware that perfection is, that God is, and good is, and love is. So, we are focusing attention on divine qualities. The qualities can be directly discerned, but the word "God" doesn't do much. It's just an intellectual concept.

Student: So, that is what you said before. That is why it is harder to understand what God is, as opposed to beauty, because we can see beauty, but we cannot see God. We have to be *aware* of God. I guess the qualities help us see God.

Dr. Hora: That's exactly right.

Student: How do we see all these spiritual qualities? There is the world, and there are all these spiritual qualities. How can I see all of these in the world? When I look at nature, beauty is easy to discern. I can see harmony, but in daily life I cannot see a lot of the qualities in individuals I meet. It is not that evident all the time. What do we see? What are we looking for?

Dr. Hora: We look for love, for joy, for intelligence, for goodness, for gratitude, for freedom, wisdom, all these qualities.

Student: We look for those qualities every day, looking to discern them. That is how we become closer to the awareness of God's presence.

Dr. Hora: Exactly.

Student: So, if we think we see a discordant event, we say, "God is present here somewhere."

Dr. Hora: But nobody notices. God is unnoticed throughout the world.

Student: So, if it is not our issue and we are observing it, is it still our responsibility to look for God in that situation, or is it just that we see the invalid idea and let it go? It is not our place to go any further?

Dr. Hora: No, we always ask, "What is the meaning of what we are seeing or what seems to be happening?"—and when you have learned to discern the meaning in situations and in the world, you then find God—right where the problem *seems* to be, there is God. There is only the good of God.

Student: When we see an ignorant idea, we can shift our attention so we are not stuck with the sense of hopelessness that we can't do anything about it.

Dr. Hora: Right. Sure. So, our student here is having a pain in her ribs, and she has a choice either to pay attention to this pain or to say, "There must be a meaning to this experience," right? The attention is turned away from the pain, because God knows nothing about pain, but God knows harmony and freedom and love. God knows these things because God *is* these things. It's not like God is a brain. God *is* the qualities, so when we say, "There is beauty, there is freedom, there is intelligence, there is goodness," we are talking about God.

Student: What she was saying was, "We have to examine what the meaning is of seeing something other than perfection."

Dr. Hora: Right. It is a great help to always ask the question "What is the meaning of what seems to be?" It is a watershed idea, which is not readily accepted in the world. Everything has a meaning.

Now, this Black fellow on the television show stood up bravely. They were yelling and screaming and didn't want to let him talk. All those bigoted people didn't want to let him have his say. He blurted out, "There is only intelligence and ignorance. There are no races. There is humanity," and of course they didn't even want to give him a chance to say that. As he stood up trying to say this, another guy behind him started yelling and screaming. It looked like he was going to jump him from behind.

It is interesting to watch these talk shows and see how people are constantly oppressing one another. Sometimes three or four people will talk at the same time and try to outshout the others. They want to prove that their point is the valid one. It is so instructive about the human condition.

Student: Some shows solicit people who are going to be very aggressive.

Dr. Hora: Yes. They invite them. Who would be interested in love and peace and wisdom? (*Laughter*)

Student: There is a woman I work with who, when we have a project to work on together, will say, "Murphy's Law, Murphy's Law, something has to go wrong." One day I was exasperated and I said, "If you invite Murphy, he will come. So, don't invite him." In dealing with individuals on projects, how do we convey—I mean, was that a right perspective? I am always so concerned about saying something that sounds preachy or...

Dr. Hora: It would have been better just to ignore it, because the meaning of her talk is to draw attention to herself, to show that she is knowledgeable. Perhaps she is a superstitious girl who wants to impress others and wants people to think that she read the book about Murphy's Law.

Student: So, would it have been better if I had asked myself what the meaning of that kind of behavior was?

Dr. Hora: You would have found out she just wanted to call attention to herself—to be considered a well-educated person.

Student: Seriousness in a workplace—is that just people who want to be important, or the idea of being known? Is that just a natural condition in a workplace?

Dr. Hora: Well, what would you call natural?

Student: Normal. It seems there is an awful lot of seriousness in the workplace.

Dr. Hora: There is nothing normal and nothing serious. These are just ignorant forms of self-confirmatory preoccupation. It's no different than a talk show, but maybe they are not yelling and screaming (*Laughter*). It is the human condition.

Other books by
Thomas Hora, M.D.

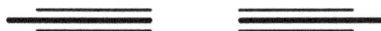

═══   ═══

ENCOUNTERS WITH WISDOM (MULTI-VOLUME SERIES)

ONE MIND

BEYOND THE DREAM

DIALOGUES IN METAPSYCHIATRY

EXISTENTIAL METAPSYCHIATRY

IN QUEST OF WHOLENESS

HEALING THROUGH SPIRITUAL UNDERSTANDING

A HIERARCHY OF VALUES

FORGIVENESS

THE SOUNDLESS MUSIC OF LIFE

CAN MEDITATION BE DONE?

COMPASSION

MARRIAGE AND FAMILY LIFE

GOD IN PSYCHIATRY

WHAT DOES GOD WANT?

SELF-TRANSCENDENCE

RIGHT USEFULNESS

COMMENTARIES ON SCRIPTURE

For more information about Metapsychiatry visit:

www.PAGL.org

The PAGL Foundation
c/o Robert Wieser
21 Talcott Road
Rye Brook, New York 10573

www.ingramcontent.com/pod-product-compliance
Lightning Source LLC
Chambersburg PA
CBHW061832040426
42447CB00012B/2937